AMERICA'S BEST IDEA

The Separation of Church and State

RANDALL BALMER

STEERFORTH PRESS
LEBANON, NEW HAMPSHIRE

This is an expanded and updated version of an earlier work
published in 2021 as *Solemn Reverence: The Separation
of Church and State in American Life.*

For information about permission to reproduce
selections from this book, write to:
Steerforth Press, 31 Hanover Street, Suite 1,
Lebanon, New Hampshire 03766

Cataloging-in-Publication Data is
available from the Library of Congress

ISBN 978-1-58642-414-5

Maufactured in the United States of America

EU RP (for authorities only): eucomply OÜ, Pärnu mnt. 139b-14, 11317,
Tallinn, Estonia, hello@eucompliancepartner.com, +33757690241

5 7 9 10 8 6 4

I contemplate with sovereign reverence that act of the whole American people which declared that their legislature should "make no law respecting an establishment of religion, or prohibiting the free exercise thereof," thus building a wall of separation between Church & State.

— Thomas Jefferson, January 1, 1802

for
John F. Wilson
(1933–2023)

No church should undertake to impose its views on public agencies, and no public agency should single out for attack any church or church organization. Under the First Amendment our government cannot — directly or indirectly, carelessly or intentionally — select any religious body for either favorable or unfavorable treatment.

— JOHN F. KENNEDY, April 15, 1960

CONTENTS

PREFACE

The First Amendment, with its insistence on the separation of church and state, religion and politics, is under attack as never before. "Congress shall make no law respecting an establishment of religion, or prohibiting the free exercise thereof," the initial clause of the First Amendment reads, and those sixteen words have served both government and faith remarkably well for more than two centuries. And yet various interests have sought in recent years to chip away at what Roger Williams, the founder of the Baptist tradition in America, called the "wall of separation" between church and state.

During the 2016 presidential campaign, for example, Donald Trump promised to repeal the Johnson Amendment, which prohibits the use of contributions to tax-exempt organizations, including religious groups, for the support of political candidates. The family of the secretary of education during the first Trump administration worked for decades to divert taxpayer money into private and religious schools, an enterprise made infinitely easier by the Supreme

Court's misbegotten *Espinoza v. Montana Department of Revenue* decision in 2020, which opened the door for taxpayer subsidies of sectarian schools. In defiance of the establishment clause of the First Amendment, the Religious Right generally has supported public prayer in public schools and the posting of religious symbols and sentiments in public places. And, both ironically and tragically, in 1979 the largest Baptist denomination in the country, the Southern Baptist Convention, effectively abandoned its historic role of patrolling the wall of separation between church and state.

I served as an expert witness in a case defending the First Amendment's prohibition against religious establishment. The trial took place in Alabama after Roy S. Moore, chief justice of the Alabama Supreme Court, placed a granite monument emblazoned with the Ten Commandments in the lobby of the judicial building in Montgomery. Had Moore allowed other religious representations in that space — or had he honored a request from the Alabama Atheists — I would have had no objection. But Moore had insisted on the Ten Commandments only, a clear violation of the establishment clause of the First Amendment, which prohibits an "establishment of religion."

My testimony then, and one reiterated in this book, is that the First Amendment is part of the genius of American life. In fact, I consider it to be America's best idea. It has protected the common good from religious factionalism, and it has ensured the integrity of faith from too close an alliance with the state.

Although unprecedented, the impetus for religious disestablishment as embodied in the First Amendment grew out of disparate impulses dating back at least to the Protestant Reformation of the sixteenth century. Martin Luther had emphasized the priesthood of believers, each individual's responsibility before God, which led almost inevitably (if not immediately) to the concession that everyone might approach God differently from his or her neighbor. The very splintering of Christianity after the Reformation demanded some sort of accommodation to its diversity. Several of the American colonies had done just that — Thomas Jefferson himself cited the examples of New York and Pennsylvania in his *Notes on the State of Virginia*, written in 1781 — though the established religions in other colonies, such as the Anglicans in Maryland and Virginia, and the Congregationalists in Massachusetts and Connecticut, stubbornly defended their establishment status. Other early voices include figures and movements such as Isaac Backus and the Separate Baptists in Massachusetts and William Livingston and the Presbyterian party in New York as influential opponents of religious establishment. Most often, however, when historians retrace the steps of religious disestablishment in America their paths lead to Roger Williams, founder of the Baptist tradition in America, and Thomas Jefferson, one of the nation's founders and the country's third president.

It's important to stipulate here at the outset that the phrase *church and state* has evolved into a kind of shorthand for understanding the relationship between two much larger, albeit amorphous, entities. One of the characteristics of the Atlantic seaboard during the colonial period was its religious diversity, ranging from Puritans in New England to Anglicans in the South. In between, groups as diverse as Baptists in Rhode Island, the Dutch Reformed in the Middle Colonies, Swedish Lutherans in Delaware, Jews in New York City, Presbyterians in New Jersey, Catholics in Maryland, and Quakers in New Jersey and Pennsylvania all established a toehold on the religious landscape of colonial America. In addition, Pennsylvania alone sheltered diverse religious minorities such as Lutherans, Mennonites, Moravians, and Schwenckfelders.

Not all groups existed in perfect harmony. The Puritan government in Massachusetts hanged Quakers on Boston Common. In 1649, Maryland, founded by Roman Catholics, passed a Toleration Act that ensured religious liberty, but it was rescinded five years later after Puritans seized control of the colony. Under Edward Hyde, Viscount Cornbury, the governor of New York, the colonial government sowed unrest in Dutch Reformed congregations as a way of preferring the Church of England. In some places, authorities sought to coerce religious uniformity and conformity. In colonial Virginia, for example, the Church of England was the established religion, and some magistrates were zealous in defense of Anglican prerogatives. Baptists, because of their insistence on religious liberty, often felt the sting of persecution. Baptists were thrown in jail in Spotsylvania in 1768 for disturbing the peace because of their preaching. A judge named Edmund Pendleton sentenced Baptist preachers to jail for what one contemporary called "the heinous charge of worshiping God according to the dictates of their own consciences." A sheriff brutally horsewhipped a Baptist minister, and a "gang of well-dressed men" nearly drowned two other Baptists by holding their heads underwater in a nearby river, a cynical riff on the Baptist insistence on believers' baptism by full immersion.

Amid all this diversity and persecution, some colonists began to warn publicly against the dangers of religious establishment. "It is not to be doubted," William Livingston, a graduate of Yale, activist in New York politics, and later the first governor of New Jersey, wrote in 1768, that "every man who wishes to be free will by all lawful ways in his power oppose the establishment of any one denomination in America." Remarking on "the inconveniences and mischiefs of religious establishments," Livingston concluded: "Religious establishments are very hardly kept from great corruption."

By the middle of the eighteenth century, it had become clear that no religious group would emerge with anything approaching hegemony. When Congress appointed a committee on July 4, 1776, to design a seal for the new nation, the committee recommended *E Pluribus Unum* — out of many, one — as the nation's motto, a nation consisting of people representing a great variety of ethnicities and religions.

The First Amendment emerged from this multicultural miasma. Even if the founders wanted to establish a "church," which would it be? As a consequence, in the place of a dominant single institution (a "church"), multiple groups and associations attempted to make claims to authority, especially in the early national period. This process produced the marketplace of religious associations, movements, and institutions that we have generally called religious pluralism.

On the political side, state, federal, and administrative institutions have undertaken to coexist while sharing political power (and authority) in contested ways. The phrase *church and state* remains useful, but what we really have is multiple religious movements and organizations confronting several layers and levels of political movements and structures. In sum, this presents us with a dynamic "system" that defies easy description. It is, rather, a messy set of shifting alignments attempting to frame the exercises of power legitimated by disparate claims to religious and political authority.

As should be clear by now, I'm a historian, not a legal scholar. Volumes and volumes have been written by lawyers and legal experts about the First Amendment and the meaning of various cases decided by the Supreme Court over the decades. This book is not an addition to that corpus; I defer to those experts and their technical analyses. Instead, as a student of American religious history, I offer here some reflections on the First Amendment and the relationship between church and state — those complicated, amorphous entities — throughout American history.

Were I to identify a foil for this book, it would be those voices breezily claiming that the United States is, and always has been, a Christian nation. That assertion is demonstrably false. Those same voices have sought, and continue to seek, a diminution of the First Amendment and its wall of separation between church and state. That, in my view, is a dangerous course. I say that not as a secularist trying to root out all expressions of religion but as someone who believes along with Roger Williams that religion functions best from the margins and not in the councils of power, that the integrity of the faith suffers from too close an association with the state.

The First Amendment has been resilient over the years, over the decades. But that does not mean that its future is secure. Those who believe in the separation of church and state must continue to patrol that wall of separation. Some on the left argue that voices of faith have no place in the arena of public discourse, while those on the right don the mantle of victim, insist that the United States is a Christian nation, and engage in rhetorical Kabuki to assert that the First Amendment does not mandate the separation of church and state.

Both positions represent misunderstandings of the First Amendment, so it's important to set the record straight. The long sweep of American history amply demonstrates the genius of the First Amendment, this grand experiment of constructing a government without the interlocking apparatus of an established religion.

1

TRANSATLANTIC VISIONARIES

In the bleak New England winter of 1636, a solitary figure trudged through the snow. Roger Williams, born in London and educated at Cambridge, had arrived in Boston in February 1631 as part of the "Great Migration" of Puritans seeking refuge from the religious oppressions of William Laud, bishop of London, and the English Crown. These Puritans were responding to John Winthrop's summons to construct a "city on a hill" in Massachusetts to show England how to configure church and state. Roger Williams wanted to be part of that scheme, and Winthrop's journal reported the arrival of Williams, describing him as "a godly minister." By 1634, Williams had settled in as the Puritan minister in Salem.

Very quickly, however, Williams ran afoul of Puritan authorities because of his suspicions of too close an association between church and state, religion and politics. In 1635, the General Court of Massachusetts brought charges against him for holding "diverse, new, and dangerous opinions," specifically for disrupting the social and religious order of New England by proposing that the church at Salem separate completely from the other Massachusetts churches. The General Court banished Williams from the colony on pain of execution, where-upon he fled south toward Narragansett Bay in January 1636, an excruciating journey of fourteen weeks in the course of which, Williams wrote, he did not know "what Bread or Bed did meane."

Williams's painful exile deepened his antipathy toward religious establishments. When he reached Narragansett Bay, he purchased land from the Narra-gansett Indians and founded Providence because of his "sense of God's merciful providence unto me in my distress." Williams determined from the outset that the new settlement "might be a shelter for persons distressed for conscience."

Williams's own conscience on matters of religion led him in the direction of Baptist ideas, which included adult (or believers') baptism and liberty of conscience, or "soul liberty." At Providence in March 1639, Ezekiel Holliman baptized Williams by full immersion at the mouth of the Mooshasuck River; Williams in turn baptized Holliman and ten others, thereby founding the Baptist tradition in North America.

Williams returned to England in 1643, during the English Civil Wars, to secure a charter for the colony of Rhode Island. While in London, responding to a letter from John Cotton, Puritan minister in Massachusetts, Williams set out his views regarding the relation of church and state in a treatise titled *The Bloudy Tenent of Persecution for Cause of Conscience*. "When they have opened a gap in the hedge or wall of separation between the garden of the church and the wilderness of the world," Williams wrote, "God hath ever broke down the wall itself, removed the candlestick, and made His garden a wilderness, as at this day." Williams sought to protect religion from the depredations of the state, and he saw strict separation as the way to accomplish this. If God, Williams believed, "will ever please to restore His garden and paradise again, it must of necessity be walled in peculiarly unto Himself from the world; and that all that shall be saved out of the world are to be transplanted out of the wilderness of the world, and added unto His church or garden."

In this memorable metaphor, Williams wanted to segregate the "garden of the church" from the "wilderness of the world" by means of a "hedge or wall of separation." Those images have become so familiar that they may have lost some of their meaning, and to understand the significance of that metaphor we must recall that the Puritans did not share our idyllic, post-Thoreauvean romantic notions about wilderness. For the Puritans of the seventeenth century, struggling to carve a godly society out of the howling wilderness of Massachusetts, wilderness was a place of danger. It was a realm of darkness where evil lurked. So when Williams wanted to protect the "garden" of the church from the "wilderness" of the world, he was concerned about preserving the integrity of the faith from defilement by too close an association with the state. Williams worried that the faith would be trivialized and fetishized when conflated with the state.

Williams's argument for religious toleration was radical, unprecedented in Western culture. Invoking the golden image of Daniel 2, Williams, addressing the Westminster Assembly in London in 1644, wondered if the idolatry decried by the Hebrew prophets wasn't a type "of the several national and state religions that all nations set up." Ultimately, however, he was persuasive: Parliament issued a charter for what became the State of Rhode Island and Providence Plantations on March 14, 1644. Rhode Island would become a laboratory not only for liberty of conscience on religious matters but also for democracy itself. "I infer that the sovereign, original, and foundation of civil power lies in the people," Williams wrote, adding that the governments they establish "have no more power, nor for no longer time, than the civil power or people consenting and agreeing shall betrust them with."

Williams's treatise, *The Bloudy Tenent of Persecution*, was published after Williams had returned to America. The ideas in the book proved so controversial that Parliament initially ordered it burned, but another edition soon appeared. By the time Williams returned to England in 1663, the controversy had passed, and Charles II had reclaimed the throne for the Stuarts. Williams sought and obtained a confirmation of the charter, which explicitly stated that no one was to be "molested, punished, disquieted, or called in question, for any differences in opinion, in matters of religion."

Whereas Williams used his "lively experiment" in North America to secure concessions from the English government, William Penn, the other transatlantic visionary of the seventeenth century, used his government connections in England to launch a "holy experiment" in the Middle Colonies. Since the late 1660s, Penn had been advancing theories about the importance of individual conscience, warning magistrates that "their authority cannot reasonably extend beyond the end for which it was appointed, which being not to enthrone themselves sovereign moderators in causes purely conscientious." Government, Penn believed, should tend to civil matters only, not religious.

In 1681, Penn, a Quaker, secured a royal charter to form "an ample colony . . . in the parts of America not yet cultivated and planted." As proprietor, Penn drew on his extensive contacts with religious dissenters in England and Europe to lure "sober people of all sorts" to his "holy experiment" in religious toleration. Before he even set foot in North America, Penn promised the settlers already there a democratic government. "For you are now fixed at the mercy of no governor that comes to make his fortune great," Penn wrote, "you shall be governed by laws of your own making and live a free, and if you will, a sober and industrious life."

And they came. Penn's "holy experiment" harbored a variety of religious and ethnic groups, including Swedes, Dutch, Germans, Scots, and French as well as Anglicans, Lutherans, Presbyterians, Baptists, and (of course) Quakers. By 1692, Pennsylvania even tolerated the public celebration of the Roman Catholic mass, the only American colony to do so. In the early decades of the eighteenth century, a variety of smaller groups also found their way to Pennsylvania: Moravians, Schwenck-felders, Dunkers, and Mennonites.

Complete harmony was elusive, even in the "holy experiment." But religious tensions were remarkably muted, at least by the standards of other colonies, and Penn's government itself did not engage in religious persecution.

Both Penn's "holy experiment" and William's "lively experiment" provided models for the configuration of church and state. Williams acted on his principles when he left Massachusetts. The colony that became Rhode Island became a place of religious toleration, a "lively experiment" where liberty of conscience and the rights of minorities would be respected. Penn spent limited time in his colony, but his vision of a place of religious pluralism and toleration stamped the character of Pennsylvania well into the eighteenth century.

Williams, Penn, and their ideas about toleration inflected more than religion; their capacious sentiments extended also to their treatment of Native Americans, a disposition that, tragically, was never adopted by the remainder of the colonies or by the nation itself. The governments of both Penn and Williams were notable for their humane treatment of Native Americans. Williams learned native languages, purchased land from the Narragansetts, and enjoyed cordial relationships with Indians throughout New England. Similarly, after Penn's arrival in the New World, he purchased land from the Lenni-Lenape, and the relations between colonial Pennsylvania and the Delaware Indians were marked by civility and mutual respect.

The transatlantic visionaries Roger Williams and William Penn bequeathed much to American life, especially their notions about religious toleration and liberty of conscience, which they linked with democracy itself.

Those ideas, leavened by John Locke's *Letter Concerning ing Toleration*, published in 1689, provided a template for religious disestablishment and the configuration of church and state formulated by the founders in the First Amendment.

2

THE FLUSHING REMONSTRANCE, WILLIAM LIVINGSTON, AND KING'S COLLEGE

Founded by the Dutch in 1624, New Amsterdam served principally as a trading entrepôt for the Dutch West India Company, and from its earliest days the town (and all of New Netherland) was religiously diverse. "At the first administration of the Lord's Supper which was observed, not without great joy and comfort to many," Jonas Michaëlius, the first Dutch Reformed minister in the colony, reported in 1628, "we had fully fifty communicants, Walloons and Dutch, a number of whom made their first confession of faith before us."

When the director-general of the colony, Pieter Stuyvesant, sought to quash religious expressions other than the Dutch Reformed Church, especially the Society of Friends (Quakers), the citizens of Flushing responded on December 27, 1657, with the Flushing Remonstrance, one of the earliest statements of religious liberty in the American colonies. "Wee desire therefore in this case not to judge least we be judged, neither to condemn least we be condemned, but rather let every man stand or fall to his own Master," they wrote, pleading for freedom of "conscience betwixt God and our own souls; the powers of this world can neither attach us, neither excuse us, for if God justifye who can condemn and if God condemn there is none can justifye."

Significantly, the thirty petitioners, none of whom was a Quaker, appealed to the laws of the Dutch Republic, the most diverse and tolerant country in the seventeenth century. The Remonstrance made it clear that all religions, not only Christianity, should enjoy freedom of religion: "The law of love, peace and liberty in the states extending to Jews, Turks and Egyptians, as they are considered sons of Adam, which is the glory of the outward state of Holland, soe love, peace and liberty, extending to all in Christ Jesus, condemns hatred, war and bondage."

Stuyvesant was unmoved. He arrested four signatories — the sheriff and town clerk of Flushing along with two other magistrates; all of them apologized and promised "to offend no more in that way." When John Bowne, an Englishman, hosted a Quaker meeting four years later, the director-general had him arrested. After Bowne refused to pay the fine that Stuyvesant had levied, Bowne, who spoke no Dutch, was banished from New Netherland. He arrived in England and then made his way to the Netherlands and appealed to the

Dutch West India Company, which found in his favor and dispatched him back to New Netherland in 1663 with a message for Stuyvesant. The Dutch West India Company instructed the director-general that "peoples' conscience should not be forced by anyone," provided that every individual "is modest and behaves in a lawful manner and therefore does not disturb others or oppose the government."

The principle of liberty of conscience in matters of religion thereby gained a toehold in New Netherland. The following year, however, the English Conquest of 1664 brought the colony under control of the English. New Netherland and New Amsterdam became New York, named for the Duke of York.

Lower-class Dutch resisted the new government, although Dutch merchants and the Dutch Reformed clergy generally cooperated with the English. Citizens had enjoyed greater rights under Dutch rule, so as the English consolidated their hold on the colony, and the Church of England sought to enjoy the advantages of state sanction, various citizens resisted the encroachment on their rights. No voice was louder or more influential than that of William Livingston.

Born in Albany, New York, in 1732, Livingston was scion of the venerable Livingston family of Livingston Manor in the Hudson River Valley, although he ridiculed "the Vanity of Birth and Titles." He was baptized into the Dutch Reformed Church, reared by his maternal grandmother, and spent a year with Henry Barclay, a Yale graduate and missionary to the Mohawks. In 1737, at the age of thirteen, Livingston matriculated at Yale, and upon his graduation four years later he studied law in New York City. He passed the bar and about that time became a Presbyterian.

With John Morin Scott and William Smith, Jr., Livingston formed the triumvirate of New York politics, fighting against the prerogatives of the Church of England and criticizing and lampooning the De Lancey party, which defended the Anglicans. Defenders of the Church of England did not take kindly to these efforts. An Anglican loyalist characterized the triumvirate as "determined, if possible, to pull down Church and State, to raise their own Government and religion upon its ruins, or throw the whole province into anarchy."

In 1748, the triumvirate organized the Society for the Promotion of Useful Knowledge, ostensibly a literary club, to propagate their ideas. They published the *Independent Reflector*, New York's first magazine and a conduit for their anticlerical and republican ideology. In its pages Livingston attacked "the Popes and Persecutors of all Churches, whether they be Popes of Rome, England, Holland or Geneva."

The formation of a college in New York provided Livingston his opportunity to weigh in on the relationship between church and state. As a graduate of Yale, Livingston advocated for a college that would enrich the cultural and educational opportunities of New York and thereby boost the colony toward parity with Massachusetts (Harvard), Connecticut (Yale), and New Jersey (Princeton). The Anglicans also supported a college, and the New York assembly authorized a series of public lotteries to raise funds for that purpose. When a board of trustees was constituted in 1751 for King's College, the nascent institution, its composition reflected the alignment of religious and political powers in the colony: one Presbyterian (Livingston himself), two Dutch Reformed, and seven Anglicans, despite the fact that Anglicans constituted only 10 percent of the population.

Trinity Church, in Lower Manhattan, contributed to the cause in 1752 by donating a valuable tract of land in the expectation that it "would be a Means of obtaining some Priviledges to the Church." Specifically, Trinity Church stipulated that Anglican liturgy would be used in religious services at the college and that Samuel Johnson of Connecticut, an Anglican, would be named president.

Livingston objected — not to the school itself, but to its sectarian character. Taking to the pages of the

Independent Reflector, Livingston characterized the
religiously inflected proposal as "a Door to universal
Bigotry and Establishment in Church, and Tyranny
and Oppression in the State." Anticipating the emphasis
on civic republicanism that would energize the Revolutionary generation a couple of decades later, Livingston believed that education should prepare students
for responsible citizenship, "a public Spirit and Love of
their Country."

Most important, a religious college would be using
public money: the lottery funds raised by the state. If
indeed the college was meant "for the public Benefit," Livingston argued, it must not be sectarian lest it
become "destructive to the civil and religious Rights
of the People." Livingston's concern was not only that
religion would be sponsored by the state but that the
state would be taking an interest in matters of faith.
Any magistrate who intervenes in religion, Livingston wrote, "exceeds the Bounds of his Authority, and
takes Cognizance of what was never submitted to his
Jurisdiction."

Livingston's opposition to the use of lottery funds did
not make him popular with the Anglican party of New
York, which managed to retaliate by suppressing the
Independent Reflector. Nevertheless, Livingston's argument prevailed; when King's College (later, Columbia

University) was chartered in 1754, the Livingston party in the legislature ensured that no public lottery funds were appropriated to support the new college. In so doing, Livingston was able to subvert what he later characterized as "the partial biggotted and iniquitous plan" for King's College.

Building on New York's long history of religious diversity dating to the seventeenth century, Livingston's opposition to the use of public funds for a sectarian school established an important precedent for church–state relations. Livingston, who became the first governor of New Jersey, may have considered it a modest victory at the time, but he nevertheless contributed one of the foundational bricks to the wall of separation between church and state.

3

FORGING THE FIRST AMENDMENT

James Madison had opposed the inclusion of a bill of rights in the United States Constitution. He feared that any right *not* specified could someday be denied, and he did not think that the federal government would ever become so powerful that such amendments would be necessary. He questioned, moreover, the adequacy of "parchment barriers" against the tyranny of majorities. Political pressure from the Baptists of Virginia and from Patrick Henry and George Mason, however, forced him to relent, and during his 1788 campaign for Congress, Madison promised he would support the addition of a bill of rights to the Constitution. In so doing, he finally concurred with his Virginia colleague Thomas Jefferson, who insisted in a December 1787 letter to Madison that "a bill of rights is what the people are entitled to against every government on earth, general or particular, and what no just government should refuse, or rest on inference."

Ultimately, Madison did not want to entrust the enterprise of formulating a bill of rights to others, so he turned to the task of what he called this "nauseating business of amendments." In addition, acting on his long-standing suspicion of religious establishments, he wanted to ensure that the new nation would not move in that direction. "Ecclesiastical Establishments tend to great ignorance and Corruption," Madison had written to William Bradford, Jr., in 1774, "all of which facilitate the Execution of mischievous Projects."

Madison was certainly influenced by Jefferson, a strong advocate for civil liberties, who directed Madison to various Enlightenment sources, including John Locke. Madison also considered more than two hundred proposals from state conventions, and he drew from the Virginia Declaration of Rights, the Massachusetts Body of Liberties, the English Bill of Rights, and even the Magna Carta. He drafted twelve amendments, but the first opened with the crucial matter of religious freedom and religious establishment.

What flowed from Madison's pen, as amended by the Senate and the House of Representatives, was a triumph, sixteen words in spare prose that set a new course for religion and politics, church and state: "Congress shall make no law respecting an establishment of religion, or prohibiting the free exercise thereof." For perhaps the first time in history, especially in the West, a government pledged to stay out of the scrum of designating one religion as the favorite of the state, thereby guaranteeing both free exercise of religion and freedom from established religion.

The new Bill of Rights, like the Constitution itself, did not please everyone. "Many pious people wish the name of the Supreme Being had been introduced somewhere in the new Constitution," Benjamin Rush wrote in 1789, the year Congress approved the Bill of Rights. "Perhaps an acknowledgement may be made of his goodness or of his providence in the proposed amendments."

In that respect of directly invoking the deity, the Bill of Rights disappointed, and continues to disappoint, those who want references to God in the nation's charter document. Congress, however, approved the First Amendment together with the other eleven amendments and sent them to the states for ratification on September 25, 1789. Ten were ratified; the other two (one dealing with the number of representatives and the other with the compensation for members of Congress) were not. The Bill of Rights became part of the Constitution — and American life — on December 15, 1791.

The story of church and state in the United States would be far simpler if the First Amendment had settled the matter once and for all, but its interpretation has been contested ever since ratification. The First Amendment had yet to be extended to the states — the

Fourteenth Amendment, ratified in 1868, initiated that process — but even on the federal level, some confusion remained about exactly where to draw this line of separation between church and state. What about military chaplains or congressional chaplains? After he left the White House, Madison opined that the formation of a congressional chaplaincy was "a palpable violation of equal rights, as well as of Constitutional principles." The appropriation of public funds to support a chaplain, he believed, represented taxpayer support for religion. "If Religion consist[s] in voluntary acts of individuals, singly, or voluntarily associated," he wrote, "and it be proper that public functionaries, as well as their constituents should discharge their religious duties, let them like their constituents, do so at their own expense."

When John Adams, the nation's second president, declared a national day of fasting, riots broke out among some of the smaller religious groups whose members feared that the government was overstepping its bounds. Adams's declaration of two "National Fasts" emerged as an issue in the bitter presidential campaign of 1800. Jefferson, Adams's challenger, opposed the idea of a national fast day. Years later, Adams attributed his defeat in 1800 to the fast days. "The National Fast, recommended by me turned me out of office," he wrote to Benjamin Rush in 1812. The declaration, Adams acknowledged, alienated

"Quakers, Anabaptists, Mennonists, Moravians, Sweden-borgians, Methodists, Catholicks, protestant Episcopa-lians, Arians, Socinians, Armenians."

Adams's acknowledgment of religious pluralism underscores both the necessity of disestablishment as well as the challenge of marking the precise line of separation between church and state. Whereas Adams saw no constitutional impediment to the proclamation of fast days, Jefferson, his successor, believed that "civil powers alone have been given to the President of the US. and no authority to direct the religious exercises of his constituents."

The disagreement between Adams and Jefferson over fast days prefigured the contestations over the interpretation of the First Amendment that would characterize discussions about church and state throughout American history. The meaning and the intent of the First Amendment are clear enough, but Americans have been debating the particulars of its application ever since.

4

GEORGE WASHINGTON AND DIVINE PROVIDENCE

George Washington came from a tobacco-growing family. He served as a commander in the Seven Years' (French and Indian) War, and as the colonists headed toward revolution, the Continental Congress persuaded the reluctant Virginian to command the Continental army. Having led the ragtag colonists to victory, Washington emerged as the consensus choice to become the nation's first president, even though he would have preferred to return to a quiet life at Mount Vernon. His misgivings surfaced in a letter to a friend: "I feel very much like a man who is condemned to death does when the time of his execution draws nigh." Washington was elected president in 1789, the only president in history to be elected unanimously by the Electoral College.

As a young man, Washington had joined the Masons, a secret fraternal order that claims a history dating to the cathedral builders of medieval Europe. In matters of faith, Washington, who was not conventionally religious, nevertheless understood the importance of religious toleration. "I trust the people of every denomination will be convinced that I shall always strive to prove a faithful and impartial patron of genuine, vital religion," Washington wrote to the Methodist bishops in 1789. "No one would be more zealous than myself to establish effectual barriers against the horrors of spiritual tyranny and every species of religious persecution."

Washington sought to live by those ideals. When he commissioned Benedict Arnold to undertake a military campaign to persuade the people of Québec, predominantly Roman Catholic, to cooperate in resisting the British, Washington had instructed Arnold to show religious toleration. "Contempt of the Religion of a Country by ridiculing any of its Ceremonies or affronting its Ministers or Votaries has ever been deeply resented," he wrote. "You are to be particularly careful to restrain every Officer and Soldier from such Imprudence and Folly and to punish every Instance of it." Having warned against intolerance, the general continued: "On the other hand, as far as lays in your power, you are to protect and support the free Exercise of the Religion of the Country and the undisturbed Enjoyment of Conscience in religious Matters, with your utmost Influence and Authority."

Arnold's military campaign to Québec failed in its mission to enlist the Canadians in the struggle against

Britain. Canada would remain British, but Washington nevertheless had established the point that the cause of American liberty would include freedom of religion.

Washington was baptized into the Church of England, but never confirmed. He served as a vestry member in his local parish, but rarely or never took Holy Communion. Many historians consider him a deist — someone who believes in a divine Creator, but a Creator who remains indifferent to his creation. In a 1776 letter to William Gordon, Washington wrote: "No Man has a more perfect Reliance on the alwise, and powerful dispensations of the Supreme Being than I have nor thinks his aid more necessary."

For a man of his time, he harbored remarkably inclusive, or "catholic," views of other religions; in 1784, for example, Washington directed his surrogate at Mount Vernon to hire "good workmen, they may be from Asia, Africa or Europe; they may be Mahometans [Muslims], Jews, Christians of any sect, or they may be Atheists." Like other founders, especially Thomas Jefferson, Washington disliked religious factionalism. "Of all the animosities which have existed among mankind, those which are caused by difference of sentiments in religion appear to be the most inveterate and distressing, and ought most to be deprecated," Washington wrote in 1792. "I was in hopes that the enlightened and liberal policy, which has marked the present age, would at least have reconciled Christians of every denomination so far that we should never again see the religious disputes carried to such a pitch as to endanger the peace of society."

For Washington and many other founders, direct references to God did not come easily; they preferred to talk about divine providence. For Washington, nothing demonstrated the workings of divine providence more dramatically than the West Point affair, a fortuitous event that once again involved Benedict Arnold. In 1779, Washington gave Arnold command of the vital West Point stronghold on the Hudson River north of New York City. Arnold, however, was a traitor; he devised a plot to turn West Point over to the British and gave the papers detailing his plan to a spy named John André, who disguised himself in an American uniform and rushed with the plans toward British headquarters in New York.

The next morning a wandering group of American soldiers, absent without leave from the Continental army, stopped André for no apparent reason. They searched him and discovered the papers, thereby foiling Arnold's treasonous plot. "In no instance, since the commencement of the war," Washington recounted, "has the interposition of Providence appeared more remarkably conspicuous than in the rescue of the post and garrison of West Point from Arnold's villainous perfidy."

Washington also believed that providence provided the margin of victory over the British. "I was but the humble agent of favoring heaven," Washington wrote after his Continental soldiers defeated the redcoats, "whose benign interference was so often manifested in our behalf, and to whom the praise of victory alone is due."

The invoking, and the crediting, of providence allowed Washington and the founding generation to speak with some unity on matters of religion, without being overly specific about whose God — or whose providence — they meant. Among a religiously diverse people, references to "providence" could be generic, without favoring or offending any religious group. But the invocations of providence also provided assurance that some larger entity was looking after the interests of the colonists, and incidents like the Benedict Arnold affair at West Point and crucial military victories provided much-needed affirmation. Just as John Winthrop, leader of the Puritans, believed that Massachusetts would be the "city on a hill," now the colonists began to believe that their fledgling nation enjoyed the benefits of divine providence.

Despite his relative lack of piety, however, Washington understood the importance of religious freedom. "The citizens of the United States of America have the right to applaud themselves for having given to mankind examples of an enlarged and liberal policy worthy of imitation," he wrote to members of Touro Synagogue in Newport, Rhode Island. "It is now no more that toleration is spoken of as if it were by the indulgence of one class of citizens that another enjoyed the exercise of their inherent natural rights, for happily the Government of the United States, which gives to bigotry no sanction, to persecution no assistance, requires only that they who live under its protection should demean themselves as good citizens, in giving it on all occasions their effectual support."

5

JOHN ADAMS AND THE TREATY OF TRIPOLI

At the first meeting of the Continental Congress in Philadelphia, John Adams recalled many years later, a motion to open the gathering with prayer "was opposed because we were so divided in religious sentiments — some were Episcopalians, some Quakers, some Anabaptists, some Presbyterians, and some Congregationalists — so that we could not join in the same act of worship." Samuel Adams, John Adams's cousin and a firebrand from Boston, finally rose and broke the deadlock. Pronouncing himself "no bigot," he allowed that he "could hear a prayer from any gentleman of piety and virtue, who was at the same time a friend to his country."

A local Church of England priest was summoned, and, dressed in the ecclesiastical vestments that had so scandalized the Puritans a century earlier, he "read the prayers in the established forms," according to John Adams, and then the thirty-fifth Psalm. "Plead my cause, O Lord, with them that strive with me," Jacob Duché, the priest, intoned, "fight against them that fight against me." Having just received the news that the British had unleashed an attack in Boston the previous day, the delegates found those words especially comforting, "as if heaven had ordained that psalm to be read on that morning." After reading the Psalm, Duché launched into an extemporaneous prayer, which, according to Adams, "filled the bosom of every man present." The delegates took notice. "I must confess I never heard a better prayer," Adams wrote, "or one so well pronounced."

John Adams had considered entering the ministry before opting to study law. Educated at Harvard, he served in the Continental Congress, as ambassador to Britain, and as Washington's vice president before his election as president in 1796. He served a single term, losing the 1800 election to Thomas Jefferson.

Though reared a Congregationalist, Adams became a Unitarian. He did not believe in the Trinity — the Christian doctrine, defined in the Nicene Creed, that God exists in three persons: Father, Son, and Holy Spirit. "My religion you know is not exactly conformable to that of the greatest part of the Christian World," Adams acknowledged in a letter to his wife, Abigail, in 1799. "It excludes superstition. But with all the superstition that attends it, I think the Christian the best that is or has been." Adams understood the value of religion. "I have attended public worship in all countries and with all sects and believe them all much better than no religion," he wrote to Benjamin Rush, "though I have not thought myself obliged to believe all I heard." The second president's most candid remarks about faith appeared in a letter to his son, John Quincy Adams, in 1816, long after the elder Adams had left office. "An incarnate God ! ! ! An eternal, self-existent, omnipresent omniscient Author of this stupendous Universe, suffering on a Cross! ! ! My Soul starts with horror, at the Idea, and it has stupified [sic] the Christian World. It has been the Source of almost all the Corruptions of Christianity."

Perhaps Adams's most enduring contribution to the conversation about church and state in the United States is the Treaty of Tripoli, negotiated during the Washington administration but ratified during Adams's presidency.

In the final decade of the eighteenth century, the United States, a fledgling nation, had no navy to protect its merchant ships; Britain had protected American maritime interests before the Revolutionary War, and France had done so during the Revolution. As a consequence, American merchant ships were vulnerable to privateering (state-sanctioned piracy); several vessels had been captured in the Mediterranean for ransom by the Barbary States: Algiers, Tunis, Morocco, and Tripoli. Their cargoes were confiscated, and crew members, especially Christians, were taken captive. Contemporary accounts suggest that Tunis alone harbored twelve thousand Christian slaves.

In 1796, the final full year of George Washington's presidency, the United States, through the agency of David Humphreys, negotiated the Treaty of Tripoli in an attempt to shield American merchant ships. The treaty was signed in Tripoli on November 4, 1796, and again at Algiers on January 3, 1797. Article 11 reads as follows:

> As the government of the United States of America is not in any sense founded on the Christian Religion, — as it has in itself no character of enmity against the laws, religion or tranquility of Musselmen [Muslims], — and as the said States never have entered into any war or act of hostility against any Mehomitan nation, it is declared by the parties that no pretext arising from religious opinions shall ever produce an interruption of the harmony existing between the two countries.

The Treaty of Tripoli was read aloud in the US Senate, and copies were provided for every senator. President John Adams added his endorsement:

Now be it known, That I John Adams, President of the United States of America, having seen and considered the said Treaty do, by and with the advice and consent of the Senate, accept, ratify, and confirm the same, and every clause and article thereof. And to the End that the said Treaty may be observed, and performed with good Faith on the part of the United States, I have ordered the premises to be made public; And I do hereby enjoin and require all persons bearing office civil or military within the United States, and all other citizens or inhabitants thereof, faithfully to observe and fulfill the said Treaty and every clause and article thereof.

The Senate ratified the Treaty of Tripoli unanimously, without debate, on June 7, 1797.

The language of Article 11 is pretty clear — "the government of the United States of America is not in any sense founded on the Christian Religion" — so anyone arguing that the United States *is* a Christian nation would need to explain away both Article 11 of the Treaty of Tripoli as well as the Senate's unanimous ratification of the treaty. Clearly, those who constituted the government in the early years of the new nation — the executive and legislative branches — had no quarrel with the statement that the United States was not founded on Christianity.

The rebuttals of the Christian nation crowd are tortured, but they seem to rely on quoting the entirety of Article 11 (reproduced above *in its entirety*), not merely the opening phrase: "As the government of the United States of America is not in any sense founded on the Christian Religion . . ." Fair enough. Context is always important. It's not clear to me, however, how the full article in any way changes the plain meaning of the phrase. The treaty makes the case that the United States has no "enmity" against Islam or Muslims. The treaty does not assert that the United States is a Christian nation; it states the opposite: "the government of the United States of America is not in any sense founded on the Christian Religion."

The second argument from the Christian nationalists centers on the renewal of tensions between the United States and the Barbary States — in part because Thomas Jefferson, as president, refused to continue payments to the Barbary States. The new American navy transported marines overseas to quell tensions — the event memorialized in the first line of the famous song "From the halls of Montezuma to the shores of Tripoli." A new treaty was eventually negotiated in 1805. Though similar to the 1797 Treaty of Tripoli, the new treaty did not replicate

Article 11, likely because Jefferson believed that the First Amendment had already settled — in the negative — the matter of the nation's supposed Christian origins.

The discrepancy between the two treaties, the Christian nationalists argue, is somehow significant. The 1805 treaty, they suggest, somehow mitigates, or even negates, the language of the Treaty of Tripoli that "the government of the United States of America is not in any sense founded on the Christian Religion."

The principle of Occam's razor might be invoked here. The fourteenth-century scholastic philosopher William of Occam (sometimes spelled *Ockham*) insisted on the precedence of simplicity, that "plurality should not be posited without necessity"; that is, of two competing theories, the simpler explanation should be preferred. In this case: "the government of the United States of America is not in any sense founded on the Christian Religion."

If the Christian nationalists reject Occam's razor, they still must confront Common Sense Realism, a philosophy that evangelicals of the nineteenth century adopted to help them interpret the Bible. Imported from Scotland, Common Sense Realism posits that the most obvious, "common sense" reading of a text is the correct one. Once again: "the government of the United States of America is not in any sense founded on the Christian Religion."

6

JAMES MADISON AND THE BAPTISTS

James Madison, sometimes called the father of the Constitution, was a member of Congress, drafted the Bill of Rights, and served as secretary of state. He was elected to the presidency in 1808 and reelected four years later. Like George Washington, Madison was reared an Anglican, but never confirmed. He attended the College of New Jersey and, like John Adams, briefly considered the ministry. He studied law and politics instead.

Madison's religious views are somewhat enigmatic, but he was a fierce opponent of religious establishments, a conviction he came to early in life. As a seventeen-year-old in Culpeper County, Virginia, Madison was walking with his father one day in 1768. The two men heard preaching coming from the local jail. Inside, Elijah Craig, a Baptist preacher, was declaiming from his cell. A crowd gathered, and young Madison took it all in. He didn't respond to the preacher's religious appeals, but the episode transformed him into a lifelong advocate for religious liberty. "That diabolical, hell-conceived principle of persecution rages," Madison wrote several years later. "There are, at present, in the adjacent county not less than five or six well-meaning men in close jail for publishing their religious sentiments," he continued. "I must beg you to pity me, and pray for liberty of conscience to all."

Like other founders, Madison considered religion conducive to "the moral order of the world and to the happiness of man," but he opposed the establishment of religion by the state. "Ecclesiastical establishments tend to great ignorance and corruption," he wrote in 1774, before the Declaration of Independence, "all of which facilitate the execution of mischievous projects." Madison also recognized the utility of religious diversity. "Freedom arises from the multiplicity of sects, which pervades America and which is the best and only security for religious liberty in any society," he declared to the Virginia Convention in 1778. "For where there is such a variety of sects, there cannot be a majority of any one sect to oppress and persecute the rest."

It was Madison's *Memorial and Remonstrance* that would turn the tide against Patrick Henry's attempt to establish Christianity in Virginia, even though Madison characterized Christianity as the "best & purest religion." Ever since its founding, the government of Virginia had been closely intertwined with the Church of England, but as the war continued, the political leaders in Virginia began to consider a different configuration. Virginia, like many of the other colonies, was venturing into new territory. Some of the colonies (Rhode Island, New York, and Pennsylvania, among others) effectively had no state church, but others (like Massachusetts, Connecticut, and Virginia) clung to their religious establishments, even if they made the designation more generic. The constitution of South Carolina, for example, stipulated that the "Christian Protestant Religion shall be deemed, and is hereby constituted and declared to be the established religion of this State."

The initial draft of the Virginia Declaration of Rights, written by George Mason, included a clause that guaranteed toleration of all religious expression: "all men should enjoy the fullest toleration in the exercise of religion, according to the dictates of conscience, unpublished and unrestrained by the magistrate." Madison, however, who had been so scandalized by the government's treatment of Baptists, thought that Mason's proposal did not go far enough. The notion of toleration, in fact, struck Madison as condescending, even paternalistic, because it inferred that the entity granting toleration — whether religion, government, or an individual — had the authority to grant toleration. Madison disagreed, recognizing that if toleration can be granted, it could also be withdrawn. This violated John Locke's notion of natural rights, that rights were inherent and not bestowed by any human entity.

Some ministers, Baptists in particular, agreed. "Government should protect every man in thinking and speaking freely, and see that one does not abuse another," wrote John Leland, a Baptist preacher who had befriended Thomas Jefferson during his time in Virginia. "The liberty I contend for is more than toleration. The very idea of toleration is despicable; it supposes that some have a pre-eminence above the rest to grant indulgence, whereas all should be equally free, Jews, Turks, Pagans and Christians."

Madison quietly set about rewriting Mason's draft. The final version of the Virginia Declaration of Rights, adopted in 1776, asserted: "That religion, or the duty which we owe to our Creator, and the manner of discharging it, can be directed only by reason and conviction, not by force or violence; and therefore all men are equally entitled to the free exercise of religion, according to the dictates of conscience; and that it is the mutual duty of all to practice Christian forbearance, love, and charity toward each other." Freedom, Madison insisted in agreement with Leland, was superior to toleration, a principle that Madison and the founders would eventually enshrine into the First Amendment. "I will not condescend to employ the word Toleration," John Adams reflected many years later. "I assert that unlimited free-dom of religion, consistent with morals and property, is essential to the progress of society and the amelioration of the condition of mankind."

Madison's emendations represented a step forward for religious liberty, but the clause had also specified the centrality of Christianity to any scheme of social order: "it is the mutual duty of all to practice Christian forbearance, love, and charity toward each other."

It was this preferment of Christianity that would provide Madison with one of his greatest challenges. In Virginia, Patrick Henry had been persuaded by argu-ments against supporting any one religious denomina-tion, even his own Church of England, the established church of the colony of Virginia. As an attorney, he had defended both Quakers and Baptists; in one memorable summation, he thundered that "Heaven decreed that man should be free — free to worship God according to the Bible." But Henry also believed that religion was an essential component of morality, and therefore the government should provide support for Christianity.

On the face of it, Henry's proposed Bill Establish-ing a Provision for Teachers of the Christian Religion represented a logical compromise between an estab-lished church and no public support whatsoever for any particular religion. He argued that the "general diffusion of Christian knowledge hath a natural tendency to correct the morals of men, restrain their vices, and preserve the peace of society." He also asserted that a tax for the support of Christianity could be enacted "without counteracting the liberal principle heretofore adopted and intended to be preserved by abolishing all distinctions of pre-eminence amongst the different societies or communities of Christians."

Henry, a fiery orator best known for his "give me liberty or give me death" speech, was a popular figure in Virginia, having been elected governor five times. Madison and Jefferson, both of whom opposed Henry's designation of Christianity as the state religion, faced an uphill political battle. Fearing that the assembly would quickly pass the bill, Madison prevailed on the legislators to postpone action to allow the proposal to circulate among the people of Virginia.

Popular reactions were mixed. "The Episcopal people are generally for it," Madison reported to James Monroe in April 1785. "The laity of the other sects are generally unanimous on the other side." That alignment might have been predicted, but Madison was especially miffed at the Presbyterian clergy, who had opposed the Anglican establishment in years past but were now "ready to set up an establishment" from which they would benefit. They were as prepared, Madison wrote disapprovingly, "to set up an establishment which is to take them in as they were to pull down that which shut them out."

The general committee of Baptists, on the other hand, true to their tradition of religious liberty and wary of state interference in matters of faith, resolved "to oppose the law for a general assessment." A subsequent gathering of this group, meeting in Powhatan, reiterated Baptist opposition, arguing that it was "repugnant to the spirit of the gospel for the Legislature thus to proceed in matters of religion." The resolution affirmed that "every person ought to be left entirely free in respect to matters of religion."

As handbills containing the text of Henry's proposed legislation circulated throughout Virginia, democracy took its course. "The printed bill has excited great discussion," Madison reported. Only a month after his earlier letter to Monroe, Madison detected a change in popular sentiments. "The adversaries to the assessment begin to think the prospect here flattering to their wishes," he wrote. Even the Presbyterian clergy were reconsidering their earlier support, "either compelled by the laity of that sect or alarmed at the probability of farther interference of the Legislature, if they begin to dictate in matters of religion."

Madison himself was hardly silent on the matter. He drafted an argument against Henry's bill, his *Memorial and Remonstrance Against Religious Assessments*, which would become a classic statement of opposition to religious establishment and a defense of religious liberty. "Who does not see that the same authority by which we can establish Christianity, in exclusion of all other religions, may establish with the same ease any particular sect of Christians, in exclusion of all other sects?" Madison asked. The majoritarianism implicit in Henry's argument that Christianity should receive state support because it was the faith of a majority of Virginians, Madison argued, was perilous because of the fact that "the majority may trespass on the rights of the minority." Madison's *Memorial and Remonstrance* linked religious establishments with the sort of tyranny that the colonists had only recently resisted. "Torrents of blood have been spilt in the old world, by vain attempts of the secular arm to extinguish religious discord, by proscribing all difference in religious opinions," he wrote. Historically, religious establishments "have been seen upholding the thrones of political tyranny," he argued; "in no instance have they been seen the guardians of the liberties of the people." Religion, Madison wrote, "must be left to the conviction and conscience of every man; and it is the right of every man to exercise it as these may dictate."

In addition to Madison's *Memorial and Remonstrance*, Virginians themselves weighed in on Patrick Henry's proposal; more than eleven thousand signed petitions in opposition to Henry's assessment to support Christianity. The measure failed, and the following year, on January 16, 1786, Virginia adopted Jefferson's *Statute for Religious Freedom*, which ensured that "no man shall be compelled to frequent or support any religious worship, place, or ministry whatsoever" and promised that "all men shall be free to profess, and by argument to maintain, their opinions in matters of religion."

Jefferson famously directed that the statute, together with the Declaration of Independence and the founding of the University of Virginia, be noted on his tombstone as his most significant accomplishments. But Madison's *Memorial and Remonstrance* was a necessary precursor to Jefferson's *Statute for Religious Freedom*. Had Madison not blocked Patrick Henry's attempt to designate Christianity as the official religion of Virginia, Jefferson's remarkable legislation would likely not have been enacted.

Years later, Madison reflected on the benefits of church–state separation. Both personal piety and civil society, he wrote in 1819, had been "manifestly increased by the total separation of the Church from the State."

7

THOMAS JEFFERSON, THE FIRST AMENDMENT, AND THE MAMMOTH CHEESE

The First Amendment was very much on Thomas Jefferson's mind on New Year's Day, 1802. As he sat down to catch up on his correspondence, the president came across a letter dated October 7 of the previous year and signed by Nehemiah Dodge, Ephraim Robbins, and Stephen S. Nelson on behalf of a group of Baptists from Danbury, Connecticut. A year before that, when Jefferson was running against the incumbent president, John Adams, Jefferson's heterodoxy was very much an issue, especially among the Federalists in New England, who feared the loss of Congregationalism as the preferred religion in Massachusetts and Connecticut. The occasion of the letter from the Baptists in Danbury, Connecticut, was to express support for the new president's efforts to extend religious disestablishment to the states. "Our sentiments are uniformly on the side of religious liberty," the Baptists wrote, "that Religion is at all times and places a matter between God and individuals; that no man ought to suffer in name, person, or effects on account of his religious opinions."

Jefferson received the letter on December 30, 1801. He sought advice from Levi Lincoln, his attorney general, and from Gideon Granger, the postmaster general. Jefferson saw the Danbury letter as an opportunity to affirm his support for the separation of church and state and also to explain why he did "not proclaim fastings & thanksgivings, as my predecessors did." The president recognized that the New England clergy, who had overwhelmingly opposed him in the presidential election, would also oppose his views on the First Amendment: "the advocate for religious freedom is to expect neither peace nor forgiveness from them." Granger, having reviewed Jefferson's draft, concurred. "The answer will undoubtedly give great Offence to the established Clergy of New England while it will delight the Dissenters as they are called," he wrote.

Earlier on that New Year's Day, Jefferson had received an unusual entourage at the White House. While Jefferson was spending his days at Monticello, he had befriended a Baptist neighbor, John Leland, who became one of Jefferson's most fervent supporters. Leland moved to Cheshire, Massachusetts, in 1792 and continued his ministry among the Baptists there, many of whom had come from Rhode Island. Leland enthusiastically supported Jefferson's election in 1800, rallying the town of Cheshire behind him. Early in Jefferson's first term, Leland sought to demonstrate that not all of New England opposed the Virginian.

The Baptist preacher came up with the idea of presenting the president with a local product of domestic arts as a token of the town's support and affection. Some of the residents of Cheshire, Massachusetts, had migrated from Cheshire, Connecticut, a town known for its cheese makers. Leland directed that all of the locals in Cheshire, Massachusetts, collect the milk from their cows on a single day, July 20, 1801, prepare the curds, and bring them to the farm of Elisha Brown, Jr. Brown's large cider press, with some modification, provided a cheese hoop, four feet in diameter and eighteen inches tall. Leland specifically directed that no milk from Federalist cows be allowed, "lest it should leaven the whole lump with a distasteful savour." As the whey was being pressed out of the hoop, Leland blessed the cheese, dedicated it to his friend in the White House, and led the townspeople in the singing of a hymn. The wheel of cheese bore the Jeffersonian motto, "Rebellion to tyrants is obedience to God."

A month after the pressing, the round of cheese weighed in at 1,235 pounds. Additional curds had been sufficient to produce another three rounds, each weighing seventy pounds. By early December, the "Mammoth Cheese," as it was known, was placed on a sled and carried to Hudson, New York, where it was conveyed by barge first to New York City and then (accounts differ) on to Baltimore and Washington. Leland and a friend, Darius Brown, accompanied the cheese, either in the same conveyance or by parallel route; Leland, who had long experience as an itinerant minister, preached to curious audiences along the way.

The December 30, 1801, edition of the *National Intelligencer and Washington Advertiser* recorded the arrival of the Mammoth Cheese: "Yesterday the cheese, made in Massachusetts to be presented to the President, was brought to the city in a wagon drawn by six horses." On the morning of New Year's Day, 1802, Leland presented the cheese to the president, "as a token of the esteem we bear to our chief Magistrate," along with an effusive letter of support from the people of Cheshire, Massachusetts. The declaration included appreciation for the Constitution and its "prohibition of religious tests to prevent all hierarchy."

Later that day, after entertaining members of the cabinet and foreign diplomats with a tasting of the Mammoth Cheese, Jefferson sat down and penned his famous letter to the Danbury Baptists. "I contemplate with sovereign reverence," the president wrote, "that act of the whole American people which declared that their legislature would 'make no law respecting an establishment of religion, or prohibiting the free exercise thereof,' thus building a wall of separation between church and state."

Jefferson had long been suspicious of religious establishment. Many of the colonies had persisted in their taxation of citizens to support an established church, but Jefferson disagreed, arguing that "to compel a man to furnish contributions of money for the propagation of opinions which he disbelieves and abhors, is sinful and tyrannical." Furthermore, Jefferson continued, "even the forcing him to support this or that teacher of his own religious persuasion, is depriving him of the comfortable liberty of giving his contributions to the particular pastor whose morals he would make his pattern, and whose powers he feels most persuasive to righteousness."

This confluence of events at the White House on January 1, 1802, serves to underscore the uniqueness of the First Amendment to the US Constitution. Not only was the notion of constructing a government without the interlocking authority of religion utterly unprecedented in Western history, but the First Amendment itself derived from the remarkable alliance of two unlikely camps: secular rationalists like Thomas Jefferson and evangelicals — especially Baptists — like

John Leland. The "wall of separation" metaphor can be traced to Roger Williams, founder of the Baptist tradition in America, who sought to protect the "garden of the church" from the "wilderness of the world" by means of a "wall of separation." Williams wanted to shield the "garden" of the church from the possibility of compromise because of entanglements with the state. The metaphor was picked up by James Burgh, a Scottish Whig, in the 1760s. He spoke of "an impenetrable wall of separation between things sacred and civil."

While Williams was a Puritan who became a Baptist, Jefferson, a creature of the Enlightenment, accepted elements of deism and thought the Church of England was too privileged. His most famous religious venture was to excise any mention of miracles or Jesus' divinity from the gospels; what remained was published as *The Life and Morals of Jesus of Nazareth Extracted Textually from the Gospels*, better known simply as the Jefferson Bible. He characterized his depiction of Jesus as "a paradigm of his doctrines, made by cutting the texts out of the book, and arranging them on the pages of a blank book, in a certain order of time or subject. A more beautiful or precious morsel of ethics I have never seen."

In an 1803 letter to Benjamin Rush, Jefferson wrote: "To the corruptions of Christianity I am indeed opposed; but not to the genuine precepts of Jesus himself. I am a Christian, in the only sense he wished any one to be; sincerely attached to his doctrines, in preference to all others; ascribing to himself every *human* excellence; & believing he never claimed any other." Some years later, he wrote: "I am a *real Christian*, that is to say a disciple of the doctrines of Jesus." Concurring with Benjamin Franklin, Jefferson believed that good works lay at the center of any religion worthy of the name. "My fundamental principle would be the reverse of Calvin's," Jefferson wrote to Thomas B. Parker in 1819, "that we are to be saved by our good works which are within our power, and not by our faith which is not within our power." Finally, Jefferson predicted that his fellow Americans would come to reject religious superstition generally and especially the notion of Jesus' divinity. "I trust that there is not a young man now living in the US. who will not die an Unitarian," Jefferson wrote just four years before his death.

While Williams worried about the integrity of the faith in too close association with the state, Jefferson and other founders feared the opposite, that religious factionalism would imperil the new government. "If the freedom of religion, guaranteed to us by law *in theory*, can ever rise *in practice* under the overbearing inquisition of public opinion," Jefferson wrote, "truth will prevail over fanaticism." During his term as president,

Jefferson considered the "experiment" in religious freedom that he had helped to create in the new republic and
pronounced it good precisely because it had proved conducive to political order and stability. "We have solved
by fair experiment, the great and interesting question
whether freedom of religion is compatible with order in
government, and obedience to the laws," he wrote to a
group of Virginia Baptists in 1808, the final year of his
presidency. "And we have experienced the quiet as well
as the comfort which results from leaving everyone to
profess freely and openly those principles of religion
which are the inductions of his own reason, and the seri-
ous convictions of his own inquiries."

This collusion between rationalists and evangelicals
— symbolically between Roger Williams and Thomas
Jefferson — that produced the First Amendment has
bequeathed to the United States a vibrant and salubrious religious culture unmatched anywhere in the world.
The First Amendment, just as Adam Smith predicted in
his 1776 treatise on capitalism, *The Wealth of Nations*,
set up a free market for religion, where religious entrepreneurs (to extend the economic metaphor) are free to
peddle their wares in the marketplace without either
prejudice or favoritism from the state. American history is full of examples, from Ann Lee and Joseph
Smith, Jr., to Mary Baker Eddy, Elijah Muhammad, and

Joel Osteen. Put simply and directly, religion has flour-ished in America precisely because the government (for the most part, at least) has stayed out of the religion business.

The success of this religious marketplace renders all the more confounding the episodic attempts through-out history to subvert the First Amendment by means of prescribed prayer in public schools, the display of religious symbols in public spaces, or, more recently, the use of taxpayer vouchers for religious schools. Paradox-ically, the very charter that ensured the success of reli-gion in America has at various times become a target as misguided individuals and movements have sought to enshrine Christianity as the religion of the nation.

Both Williams and Jefferson, though separated by more than a century, advocated religious disestablish-ment, albeit out of somewhat different motives. Williams saw the dangers of state interference in the church, the wilderness encroaching on the garden, while Jeffer-son recognized the dangers that religious interests and factions posed to the political order that he had so care-fully fashioned. I should like to suggest, however, that the configuration of church and state embodied in the First Amendment — the guarantee of free exercise and the proscription against religious establishment — has succeeded over the past two-plus centuries beyond even the boldest expectations of either Williams or Jefferson. This wall of separation — which more accurately resembles a line in the dust, continually drawn and redrawn — has satisfied Jefferson's concern that confessional agendas not disrupt political stability, and it has also ensured the religious vitality everywhere in evidence throughout American history.

From Monticello, more than a decade after he had left the White House, Jefferson reflected on the great American experiment of separating church and state. "Our country has been the first to prove to the world two truths, the most salutary to human society, that man can govern himself, and that religious freedom is the most effective anodyne against religious dissension," he wrote. Jefferson pointed out what many Americans, then and now, would regard as a paradox: "the maxims of civil government being reversed in that of religion, where it's [sic] true form is 'divided we stand, united we fall.'"

8

DISESTABLISHMENT IN CONNECTICUT

The First Amendment to the Constitution, which guaranteed freedom of religious expression and forswore religious establishment, was passed by Congress in 1789 and ratified by the states in 1791. Those provisions, however, did not apply immediately to the states, and two states in particular, Connecticut and Massachusetts, clung to religious establishments. Connecticut finally disestablished the Congregational Church in 1818; Massachusetts followed in 1833. The story of disestablishment in Connecticut is especially instructive.

Connecticut was founded by Puritans as the New Haven Colony. Although Congregationalists predominated, by the turn of the nineteenth century other "dissenters" had taken their place on the religious landscape: Episcopalians, Methodists, Baptists, Universalists, and the Society of Friends (Quakers). One such aggregation was the Danbury Baptist Association, formed in 1790 and consisting of twenty-six congregations. The Danbury Baptists had supported Thomas Jefferson in the election of 1800; they wrote to congratulate him and also to ascertain the president's views on religious freedom and his understanding of the Constitution.

As the state of Connecticut began to contemplate disestablishment, Lyman Beecher sounded the alarm. A graduate of Yale, Beecher served as pastor of the Congregational church in Litchfield, Connecticut, from 1810 to 1826. Beecher defended the standing order of Congregational ministers against the charge of unfair taxation to support the Congregational establishment. "The minor sects had swollen, and complained of having to get a certificate to pay their tax where they liked; our efforts to enforce reformation of morals by law made us unpopular."

As the disestablishment legislation advanced, Beecher bewailed the loss of morality should the Congregational Church lose its preferential status. "It was a time of great depression and suffering," he lamented. "It was the worst attack I ever met in my life."

The 1818 referendum on a new constitution included the stipulation that no one could "by law be compelled to join or support, nor be classes with, or associated to, any congregation, church or religious association." The votes for disestablishment prevailed, albeit by a small margin, and Beecher feared the worst. Two years later, however, amid a revival of religion, the minister changed his tune. "Revivals now began to pervade the state," he wrote in

1820. "There came such a time of revival as never before in the state." Disestablishment, Beecher added, was "the best thing that ever happened to the State of Connecticut. It cut the churches loose from dependence on state support. It threw them wholly on their own resources and on God."

Disestablishment in Connecticut demonstrates the power of the religious marketplace under the First Amendment. The separation of church and state meant that no one religious group — Congregationalists in this case — enjoyed the support and the favor of the state. Each was required to compete for funds and followers in the marketplace of religion. This religious marketplace, in turn, has lent energy and dynamism to religious life in America and has allowed for an endless stream of religious entrepreneurs.

What are the benefits of disestablishment? In Connecticut, demand for clergy rose after 1818, as did the ministers' salaries. Connecticut also saw an increase in church membership, a circumstance replicated in Massachusetts following disestablishment. By 1837, the *Christian Register* noted, "Within a few years, a vast change has taken place in the ecclesiastical condition of New England."

9

DESIGNATING THE UNITED STATES AS A "CHRISTIAN NATION"

At various times in American history, citizens have paused to notice that the US Constitution contains no direct acknowledgment of God — which is certainly an inconvenient detail for those who want to insist that America is, and always was, a Christian nation. The Confederacy seized on this during the Civil War, arguing against the legitimacy of the Union because of this apparent omission, all the while careful to ensure that the Confederate Constitution invoked "the favor and guidance of Almighty God."

Northerners who worried about this issue pointed to the Union's lack of success early in the war as evidence of divine displeasure; God was apparently judging the Union for its failure to acknowledge the Almighty in the founding documents. Meeting in February 1863, representatives from a coalition of eleven Protestant denominations from seven Northern states decided that something needed to be done to assuage divine wrath. They originally organized themselves as the

National Association to Secure the Religious Amendment of the Constitution. The organization sent a "memorial" to Congress with its proposed amendment: "We, the people of the United States, humbly acknowledging Almighty God as the source of all authority and power in civil government, the Lord Jesus Christ as the Ruler among the nations, His revealed will as the supreme law of the land, in order to constitute a Christian government, and in order to form a more perfect union, establish justice, insure domestic tranquillity, provide for the common defense, promote the general welfare, and secure the inalienable rights and the blessings of life, liberty, and the pursuit of happiness to ourselves and our posterity, and all the people, do ordain and establish this Constitution for the United States of America."

The delegation then met with President Abraham Lincoln, entreating him to endorse their proposal. Lincoln temporized, writing, "The general aspect of your movement I cordially approve. In regard to particulars I must ask time to deliberate, as the work of amending the Constitution should not be done hastily. I will carefully examine your paper in order more fully to comprehend its contents than is possible from merely hearing it read, and will take such action upon it as my responsibility to our Maker and our country demands." Although the

proposed amendment had several congressional spon-
sors, it never came up for a vote.

Undeterred, the amendment activists pressed their
case. In 1866, having taken a new name, the National
Reform Association, they circulated their "memorial"
to churches and other organizations, seeking support.
The document was signed by politicians and judges;
the faculties of Princeton Theological Seminary and
Western Theological Seminary endorsed it. Ministers
urged their congregants to write members of Congress
in support of the proposed amendment, and petitions
were circulated and sent to Washington. In 1867, the
organization added a publication, the *Christian Statesman*, to push for an amendment. A religious amendment, the *Statesman* said, "is but a means to an end, and
that end is the arousing and combining of the Christian
people of America in a compact, enthusiastic, determined movement to carry out the religious idea of
government in all its practical applications."

The movement to amend the Constitution boasted
influential supporters, including William Strong, a graduate of Yale, a Presbyterian, and a justice on the Pennsylvania Supreme Court, who was named president of
the National Reform Association. Strong was active
with the American Board of Commissioners for Foreign
Missions, served as vice president of the American Tract

Society beginning in 1871 and as president of that society starting in 1873, and was president of the American Sunday School Union beginning in 1883. He held all of these posts concurrently with his judicial service.

Following Strong's appointment to the US Supreme Court by Ulysses S. Grant in 1870, he remained as head of the National Reform Association until 1874. The organization stepped up its efforts. "The question of the Bible in the Public Schools, of Sabbath Laws, and of many similar questions are now demanding attention and decisive settlement," the association declared in 1873. "Shall the Nation preserve the Christian features of its life? This is rapidly becoming the issue of our day." The National Reform Association appealed to patriotism. "Shall we obliterate every Christian feature from existing institutions? Or, shall we make the Constitution explicitly Christian? Shall we thrust the Bible from our schools to make them conform to the Constitution? Patriotism and true Statesmanship answer, No!" The Methodist publication *Christian Advocate* endorsed the amendment.

The push for a constitutional amendment also engendered opposition. On February 28, 1872, Carl Schurz, US senator from Missouri, presented Congress with a petition with more than ten thousand signatures from across the nation "asking Congress to preserve inviolate the great guarantees of religious liberty, and protesting against an amendment to the Constitution establishing religious tests." Octavius Brooks Frothingham, a Unitarian minister, opposed the "Christian amendment" on the grounds of religious freedom and formed the National Free Religious Association. Francis Ellingwood Abbot, another Unitarian, organized the National Liberal League in 1876, which opposed the "Christian amendment," called for rescinding tax exemptions for religious organizations, condemned the reading of the Bible in public schools, and advocated for the removal of government chaplains. Twenty students at Harvard Divinity School, a redoubt of Unitarianism, signed a statement against the amendment, warning against overthrowing "the great principles of complete religious liberty and the complete separation of church and state."

As pressure increased, US senator from Massachusetts Charles Sumner presented another petition opposed to the amendment, this one with 35,179 names on a roll that stretched out nearly a thousand feet. "It is seldom that 35,000 people can be found to sign an appeal against a wise measure," the *Boston Globe* commented, "and the 953 feet of the petition certainly go a great way in demonstrating the absurdity of the proposed constitutional plan of salvation."

The National Reform Association's efforts to amend the Constitution failed. Even Roman Catholics, against whom some of the "Christian amendment" agitation had been directed, affirmed the First Amendment; the Second Plenary Council, meeting in Baltimore in 1866, declared, "Church and State, therefore, are entirely distinct and separate according to our fundamental laws."

But failure to pass a "Christian amendment" hasn't prevented succeeding members of Congress from pursuing similar, if less sweeping, legislation. In 1888, a bill was introduced "to secure to the people the enjoyment of the first day of the week, commonly known as the Lord's day, as a day of rest, and to promote its observance as a day of worship." A 1944 bill would have designated the period from Thanksgiving to Christmas every year "for Nation-wide Bible reading," and another bill three years later would have declared Good Friday a legal holiday.

These efforts very often targeted the District of Columbia, over which the Congress retained exclusive jurisdiction (Congress granted limited "home rule" to the District in 1973). In 1892, a bill was introduced to prohibit the delivery of ice on Sunday, and a 1937 bill would have mandated the Sunday closing of bowling alleys in the District of Columbia.

The next wave of efforts to designate the United States

as a Christian nation took place, unsurprisingly, in the
1940s and 1950s. In the throes of the Cold War, with
persistent worries that godless communists were poised
to take over the country either by attack, invasion, or
subversion, Congress sprang into action. A proposed
constitutional amendment, first advanced in 1947 by
a group called the Christian Amendment Movement,
would have recast the first three sections of Article I:

- **Section 1:** This nation devoutly recognizes the
  authority and law of Jesus Christ, Savior and
  Ruler of nations, through whom are bestowed
  the blessings of Almighty God.
- **Section 2:** This amendment shall not be inter-
  preted so as to result in the establishment of
  any particular ecclesiastical organization, or
  in the abridgment of the rights of religious
  freedom, or freedom of speech and press, or
  of peaceful assemblage.
- **Section 3:** Congress shall have power, in such
  cases as it may deem proper, to provide a suit-
  able oath or affirmation for citizens whose
  religious scruples prevent them from giving
  unqualified allegiance to the Constitution as
  herein amended.

Sections 1 and 2 were reminiscent of Patrick Henry's failed attempt to establish the Christian religion in Virginia.

Although the proposed amendment failed to pass, in part because of the anti-Semitic sentiments of some who argued for its passage, Congress during the Eisenhower administration pursued other means to blur, if not to eliminate, the line of separation between church and state. In February 1954, Dwight Eisenhower sat in the pews at New York Avenue Presbyterian Church as George M. Docherty advocated the addition of "under God" to the Pledge of Allegiance. "To omit the words 'under God' in the Pledge of Allegiance is to omit the definitive factor in the American way of life," Docherty said from the pulpit. He believed that "under God" was inclusive enough for Jews and Muslims, although he had no patience for atheists. "An atheistic American is a contradiction in terms," Docherty declared. "If you deny the Christian ethic, you fall short of the American ideal of life."

Eisenhower endorsed the proposal to add to the Pledge of Allegiance, which had also been advocated for some time by the Knights of Columbus. Congress soon passed a joint resolution adding the words "under God" to the Pledge of Allegiance, which Eisenhower signed on June 14, 1954. "From this day forward," the president declared, "the millions of our schoolchildren will daily proclaim in every city and town, every village and rural schoolhouse, the dedication of our nation and our people to the Almighty."

Next, the Cold War Congress targeted money. In the throes of the Civil War, Salmon Chase, secretary of the treasury, had instructed the US Mint to include some representation of divine dependence on coins "without unnecessary delay." The motto IN GOD WE TRUST appeared on the two-cent coin beginning in 1864, and the Coinage Act of 1873 directed that the secretary of the treasury "may cause the motto IN GOD WE TRUST to be inscribed on such coins as shall admit of such motto." From 1883 until 1938, however, the motto disappeared from the buffalo head nickel.

In 1956, a resolution by the Eighty-Fourth Congress designated *In God We Trust* as the national motto. The following year that motto was added to the national currency.

Supreme Court decisions on school prayer in the early 1960s, *Engel v. Vitale* in 1962 and *Abington School District v. Schempp* the following year, unleashed another round of attempts to inscribe religion into the Constitution. In 1964, Frank Becker, a member of Congress from Long Island and a Roman Catholic, introduced an amendment to ensure that "prayers may be offered in the course of any program in any public school or other public place in the United States." Becker believed that the stakes were high. "The welfare and entire future of our beloved America depends upon how we handle the most dynamic tradition in our national life," he declared, "dependence upon Almighty God." The Becker Amendment enjoyed widespread support in Congress, but it was opposed by Emanuel Celler, chair of the House Judiciary Committee and a Reform Jew. Celler was eventually forced to conduct hearings on the amendment, but he was able to delay long enough to marshal opposition, and the bill died.

In the wake of Supreme Court decisions in the early 1960s that outlawed prescribed prayer and Bible reading in public schools, Everett Dirksen, US senator from Illinois and minority leader, introduced an amendment in 1966 that read, "Nothing in the Constitution prohibited the administrator of a publicly supported school or building from 'providing for or permitting the voluntary participating by students or others in prayer.'" This proposal enjoyed widespread popular support. Dirksen said, "I can see no evil in children who want to say that God is good and to thank Him for their blessings." Citizens lobbied Congress on behalf of the amendment; Pat Boone, a celebrity, mobilized behind the effort with an initiative called Project Prayer. "Hell, I sound like Billy Graham,"

Dirksen himself declared. "I'm positively evangelical about this."

Once again, opposition mounted over questions about who would be composing the prayers that school-children would be required to pray. As Mike Mansfield, majority leader of the Senate, said, "One's religious practice is too personal, too sacred, too private to be influenced by pressures for change each time a new school board is elected." The Dirksen Amendment was supported by forty-nine senators, nine votes short of the two-thirds majority needed to pass the Senate.

The absence of a reference to God in the US Constitution has attracted the notice of activists and demagogues at various points throughout American history. The founders, recognizing the multifaith character of the emerging nation, were careful not to designate a denomination, a tradition, or even a religion as the established faith in the United States. Despite various attempts to circumvent the founders' wisdom as embodied in the First Amendment, Congress and the president have so far repulsed those efforts. As Lincoln said in fending off one such initiative, "the work of amending the Constitution should not be done hastily."

10

SCHOOL WARS AND THE BLAINE AMENDMENTS

James G. Blaine, born in West Brownsville, Pennsylvania, graduated from Washington (now Washington and Jefferson) College in Pennsylvania and moved to Augusta, Maine, in 1854 as editor and part owner of the *Kennebec Journal*, a Republican newspaper. After serving four years in the Maine legislature, Blaine was elected to the House of Representatives in 1862 and became speaker of the House in 1868. A contender for the Republican presidential nomination in 1876, he lost to Rutherford B. Hayes on the seventh ballot.

Blaine was appointed to fill a Senate vacancy and then won election to a full term. He was a contender once again for the Republican presidential nomination in 1880, and following the election of James A. Garfield, Blaine became secretary of state. Blaine finally won the nomination in 1884, but he lost the election to Grover Cleveland. He again became secretary of state in 1889, serving under Benjamin Harrison until failing health prompted his resignation in 1892. Despite his foreign policy achievements, principally in relations with Latin

American countries, Blaine is probably best known for his advocacy of what became known as the Blaine amendments, which forbade the use of taxpayer money for the support of religious, primarily Catholic, schools.

On December 7, 1875, Ulysses S. Grant first proposed a constitutional amendment barring the teaching of religion in public schools. "I suggest for your earnest consideration — and most earnestly recommend — a constitutional amendment making it the duty of each of the several States to establish and forever maintain free public schools," the president said in a message to Congress in 1875, and "forbidding the teaching in said schools of religious, atheistic, or pagan tenets." Blaine, then Republican leader in the House of Representatives and whose mother was Roman Catholic, picked up the cause a week later, proposing to bar public financing for religious, especially Catholic, schools. His joint resolution was the first bill filed in the Forty-fourth Congress on December 14, 1875.

Schools had long been a battleground for church–state contestations. The 1780 constitution for Massachusetts provided for "public protestant teachers" who would foster "piety, education, and morality." As early as the 1820s, religious groups — in this case, Methodists and Baptists — had applied for public funding. The New York Common Council, however, refused on constitutional grounds, arguing that such appropriations to "Methodist, Episcopalian, Baptist, and every other sectarian school" would promote an "unnatural union of Church and State." Members of the council's legal committee framed their objections rhetorically: "Can we, without violating the Constitution, appropriate any public funds to the support of those schools or institutions in which children are taught the doctrines and tenets of religious sectarianism?" The answer, clearly, was no.

Nevertheless, common schools, with their Protestant-inflected curricula, had been used as a means of assimilating immigrant children into American life. "Religion will tend to mold together the great majority of our people," Justin Morrill, US senator from Vermont, said, "as it is distinctly Protestant." Instruction in public schools included the inculcation of morality based explicitly on Christian teachings. But, as Morrill suggested, the curriculum was also at least implicitly — sometimes explicitly — Protestant, so much so that the Protestant bias in public schools triggered the so-called school wars in New York City, Philadelphia, and other cities. In one of the most famous confrontations, ten-year-old Thomas J. Whall, an Irish-born Catholic student at the Eliot School in Boston, had his hands beaten with a rattan stick for refusing to recite the Protestant (King

James) version of the Ten Commandments. Protestants, however, refused to give ground, linking religious instruction with public morality.

John Hughes, the Catholic archbishop of New York, was especially exercised over the use of what he considered Protestant translations of the Bible in public school classrooms coupled with the Protestant notion that anyone could interpret the Bible for himself or herself. "Besides the introduction of the Holy Scriptures without note or comment, with the prevailing theory that from these even children are to get their notions of religion, contrary to our principles, there were in the classbooks of those schools false (as we believe) historical statements respecting the men and things of past times, calculated to fill the minds of our children with errors of fact, and at the same time to excite in them prejudice against the religion of their parents and guardians." Hughes argued that these practices by the New York Public School Society were inimical to American principles. "Is this state of things, fellow-citizens, and especially Americans, is this state of things worthy of you, worthy of our country, worthy of our just and glorious constitution?" he asked. "Put yourself in the poor man's place, and say whether you would not despise him if he did not labor by every lawful means to emancipate himself from this bondage. He has to pay double taxation for the education of his child, one to the misinterpreted law of the land, and another to his conscience."

The persistence of Protestant bias in common schools led Catholics to form their own, parochial schools. Soon thereafter, Catholic voices began clamoring for taxpayer funds, in part to counter what Hughes had characterized as "double taxation." To forestall the possibility of funding for sectarian education, James Blaine's proposed constitutional amendment would have expanded the First Amendment to read, "No state shall make any law respecting an establishment of religion or prohibiting the free exercise thereof; and no money raised by taxation in any state for the support of public schools, or derived from any public fund therefor, nor any public lands devoted thereto, shall ever be under the control of any religious sect, nor shall any money so raised or lands so devoted be divided between religious sects or denominations."

The debate over the so-called Blaine amendment to the Constitution was heated. Opponents discerned what one representative called "a sinister sentiment of religious bigotry" behind efforts to deny taxpayer funds to Catholic schools. Supporters sought to ensure that "pure and undefiled religion" would continue to be taught in public schoolrooms as opposed to "the particular creeds or tenets of either religionists or infidels."

Although the measure easily passed the House of Representatives, supporters of the Blaine amendment failed to secure the two-thirds majority they needed in the Senate. Nevertheless, many states adopted their own "Blaine amendments" to prohibit the use of taxpayer funds to support sectarian schools.

In recent years, advocates of school vouchers have sought to nullify the "Blaine amendments" in various states. The state of Washington has one of the most stringent prohibitions against the use of taxpayer funds for religious education; the relevant passage in the state constitution reads, "All schools maintained or supported wholly or in part by the public funds shall be forever free from sectarian control or influence." That provision came under attack after Joshua Davey was denied a state-funded Promise Scholarship because he intended to use it to pursue a theology degree. In 2004, the dispute reached the US Supreme Court in *Locke v. Davey*. The court ruled 7 to 2 in favor of the state of Washington and its refusal to fund sectarian education.

Unfortunately, in 2020 the Supreme Court, its conservative majority newly fortified with two Donald Trump appointments, reversed course in *Espinoza v. Montana Department of Revenue*, not only weakening the establishment clause but also opening the way for the nullification of Blaine amendments across the country. Writing for the 5 to 4 majority, John G. Roberts, Jr., the chief justice, prepared the way for public funding of private education, including sectarian schools. "A state need not subsidize private education," he wrote. "But once a state decides to do so, it cannot disqualify some private schools solely because they are religious."

11

MORMONS AND THE "DIVINE ORIGINS" OF THE CONSTITUTION

In all of American history, no religious group has had a more contested relationship with the US government than the Mormons. Joseph Smith, Jr., born in Vermont in 1805, moved with his family to Palmyra, New York, in 1816, a region convulsed with religious unrest. Smith's restless spirit eventually led him to the woods in 1820, where he had his "first vision" — a visitation from God the Father and Jesus — and eventually to Hill Cumorah, where on September, 22, 1827, Smith claimed to find the golden tablets that he translated into the *Book of Mormon*. Following its publication in 1830, Smith organized a small group of believers in Fayette, New York, into what later became known as the Church of Jesus Christ of Latter-day Saints.

The story of the Mormons in the nineteenth century is one of relentless persecution, displacement, and adjustment. Local opposition forced Smith and his followers from Fayette, New York, to Kirtland, Ohio, in 1831. The following year, Smith was tarred and feathered, allegedly for making passes at a teenage girl. The failure of the Kirtland Bank in 1837 further antagonized non-Mormon ("gentile") neighbors, and Smith increasingly cast his eyes on Missouri as a new home for his fledgling religion; Smith himself finally left Ohio for Missouri in 1838.

As early as 1831, Smith had designated Jackson County, Missouri, as the site of the biblical Zion, even though he did not step foot in the state until several years later. His followers began gathering in Caldwell County, Missouri, but once again they faced opposition, this time not only from neighbors but also from the governor. "Gentiles" resented Mormon settlement and tried to prevent the Latter-day Saints from voting, thereby setting off the Mormon War of 1838 in Caldwell and neighboring counties. On October 27, 1838, Governor Lilburn Boggs issued his infamous Executive Order 44, also known as the Extermination Order, which read in part: "the Mormons must be treated as enemies, and must be exterminated or driven from the State if necessary for the public peace."

Emboldened by legal protection, Missourians attacked the Mormon settlement at Haun's Mill, leaving eighteen Mormons dead. Smith and others retreated to Far West, Missouri, where they were captured. As a condition of their release, the Mormons agreed to leave Missouri; they retreated across the Mississippi River to yet another new settlement, Nauvoo, chartered by the state of Illinois in 1840.

Smith soon accrued to himself political power in addition to his religious authority. He was head of the Nauvoo Legion and mayor of Nauvoo. On January 12, 1844, Smith announced his candidacy for president of the United States. Once again, however, his critics pounced. Rumors had begun to circulate in Nauvoo about Smith's polygamist practices, and when the *Nauvoo Expositor* published some of these claims in its first and only edition, June 7, 1844, Smith ordered the press destroyed. Locals were enraged, and Smith surrendered to the authorities in Carthage, Illinois, on June 25. Two days later, a mob of approximately two hundred stormed the jail and murdered Smith and his brother Hyrum.

Following a succession crisis, Brigham Young, president of the Quorum of the Twelve Apostles, emerged as leader of the Latter-day Saints. The Mormons had been looking toward the West for a while, and renewed hostility in Nauvoo prompted Young to organize one of the most remarkable migrations in American history. The Great Salt Lake Basin was in many ways an inhospitable venue, but it had the great advantage of lying outside the territory of the United States. Perhaps here, Young believed, the Mormons could flourish without fear of interference from the US government.

Young consolidated his authority as head of the Latter-day Saints and also as temporal ruler of a territory the Mormons called Deseret. His civil authority extended to law enforcement, education, and cultural affairs, and he sought to make the Mormons economically self-sufficient. He welcomed converts from abroad, and he authorized the establishment of colonies throughout present-day Utah, Nevada, Arizona, and Idaho.

The 1848 Treaty of Guadalupe Hidalgo, which concluded the Mexican–American War, brought Deseret — and the Mormons — once again into the territory of the United States. President Millard Filmore appointed Young governor of the Utah Territory and superintendent of Indian affairs.

By 1852, Young felt confident enough of the Mormons' security that he acknowledged publicly the Mormon practice of polygamy, what Smith had called "plural marriage." The reaction among "gentiles" was swift and condemnatory. The platform of the Republican Party in 1856 condemned the "twin relics of barbarism": slavery and polygamy. In 1857, President James Buchanan replaced Young as governor with Alfred Cumming, of Georgia, and dispatched federal troops to Utah.

The Mormons resisted as best they could, closing wagon trails, making treaties with Indians, disrupting military supply lines, and refusing to sell goods

to emigrants passing through. The story of the ensuing decades is one of escalating tensions between the
Latter-day Saints and the US government. Congress
passed a series of laws, beginning with the Morrill Anti-
Bigamy Act of 1862, designed to pressure Young and the
Mormons to abandon plural marriage. In *Reynolds v.
United States*, the Supreme Court ruled in 1879 that
George Reynolds's conviction on charges of bigamy was
constitutional. To permit polygamy, the chief justice
wrote, "would be to make the professed doctrines of
religious belief superior to the law of the land, and in
effect to permit every citizen to become a law unto
himself." The Edmunds Act of 1882 sought to tighten the
vise. Sponsored by George F. Edmunds, who, like Justin
Morrill, was a senator from Vermont, the Edmunds Act
declared polygamy a felony, deprived those guilty of
the right to vote, and declared them ineligible to hold
public office. In a provision aimed at closing a loophole,
it declared that "unlawful cohabitation" was illegal.

John Taylor, Young's successor as church president,
remained defiant. A polygamist himself, he went into
hiding and on September 27, 1886, claimed a revelation
from God affirming plural marriage. Congress upped
the ante the following year with the Edmunds–Tucker
Act, which legally dissolved the Mormon church and
set fines of $500 to $800 and five years in prison for

polygamy; more than thirteen hundred men (and a few women) served time in Utah, Arizona, South Dakota, Michigan, and Iowa.

With an eye on statehood for Utah, Wilford Woodruff, Taylor's successor, finally de-escalated the standoff between the Mormons and the federal government. His 1890 Woodruff Manifesto declared that the Latter-day Saints would hereafter conform to the laws of the United States. Although Mormon compliance was gradual, the new policy paved the way for Utah statehood in 1896.

Conflicts with the government, however, did not end there. B. H. Roberts was elected to Congress in 1898, but the House of Representatives refused to seat him because he was a polygamist. After Reed Smoot, member of the Quorum of the Twelve Apostles, was elected to the Senate in 1902, his seating turned into a proxy debate over plural marriage, even though Smoot himself was not a polygamist. A Senate committee recommended against seating Smoot, but the Senate overruled the recommendation; Smoot (co-sponsor of the Smoot-Hawley Tariff Act of 1930, which many historians believe exacerbated the Great Depression) served in the Senate from 1907 to 1933.

Given the persecution of the Latter-day Saints in the nineteenth century and their contested relationship with the federal government, which persisted into the twentieth century, one would think that the Mormons would have a jaundiced view of the US government. However, the *Doctrine and Covenants*, a repository of divine revelations to Joseph Smith and succeeding presidents of the church, tells a different story. Speaking in the voice of God, section 98:5 reads, "And that law of the land which is constitutional, supporting that principle of freedom in maintaining rights and privileges, belongs to all mankind, and is justifiable before me." Mormons believe that even the US Constitution is divinely inspired. Section 101:80 reads, "And for this purpose have I established the Constitution of this land, by the hands of wise men whom I raised up unto this very purpose, and redeemed the land by the shedding of blood."

Mormon leaders bow to no one in their veneration of the nation's founders or in invoking divine providence. Ezra Taft Benson, who served as secretary of agriculture to Dwight Eisenhower and later became president of the Church of Jesus Christ of Latter-day Saints, extolled the founders in an article in the *Ensign*, a church magazine. "Our Father in Heaven planned the coming forth of the Founding Fathers and their form of government as the necessary great prologue leading to the restoration of the gospel," he wrote.

Curiously, this tenet of Mormon belief has rarely surfaced in political discourse. When George Romney, the governor of Michigan and a Mormon, ran for the Republican presidential nomination in 1968, he was eager to talk about his faith. But no one at the time seemed interested in that conversation. By contrast, when his son, Mitt Romney, the former governor of Massachusetts, sought the Republican nomination forty years later, the son was pressed repeatedly about his Mormonism — though never about the divine origins of the Constitution. The younger Romney studiously evaded questions about his faith by saying, "I'm not a theologian" and "I don't speak for my church."

When he finally succumbed to pressure to address the issue, Mitt Romney continued to equivocate. In a speech at the George Bush Presidential Library in College Station, Texas, on December 6, 2007, Romney offered a paean to religious liberty, but (apparently with his eyes on the Religious Right in the upcoming Iowa precinct caucuses) refused to affirm the First Amendment and the separation of church and state. Polling later revealed that a majority of Americans professed indifference to Romney's faith, that it did not disqualify him for national office. After decades of struggle for legitimacy, Mormonism had finally won acceptance as a faith tradition in America's pluralistic religious landscape.

12

THE JOHNSON AMENDMENT AND
THE FIRST AMENDMENT

In 1954, Lyndon Johnson, then a first-term senator, was facing a tough reelection campaign in Texas. After a failed earlier attempt, Johnson had won the 1948 Democratic nomination (then tantamount to election) for the Senate by eighty-seven votes over former governor Coke Stevenson amid charges of election fraud. Friendly political machines, credible sources insisted, had mysteriously discovered just enough votes to throw the nomination to Johnson. When he arrived in the Senate the following January, his colleagues dubbed the new senator "Landslide Lyndon."

Six years later, running for reelection, Johnson wanted to take no chances. Several nonprofit groups were allied against him, claiming that he was a communist. These groups, Facts Forum and the Committee for Constitutional Government, were using their tax-exempt status to engage in McCarthy-like attacks against Johnson because they perceived him as too liberal.

Founded in 1937 to oppose Franklin Roosevelt, the

Committee for Constitutional Government by the late 1940s was spending massive sums of money, according to the *New York Times*, lobbying for "lower business taxes, more and better anti-union legislation, reduced appropriations for the Department of Labor and other Federal agencies." Facts Forum had been created in 1951 with money from H. L. Hunt, a Texas oil tycoon who believed that "the Democratic Party, except for its Dixiecrat wing, is the instrument of socialism and Communism." As the 1954 election approached, both organizations set their sights on the junior senator from Texas.

Johnson didn't want adversarial groups working against him under cover of tax-exempt organizations, so on July 2, 1954, he proposed an addition to the tax code that prohibits tax-exempt organizations from openly supporting political candidates. In the words of the tax code, "all section 501(c)(3) organizations are absolutely prohibited from directly or indirectly partic- ipating in, or intervening in, any political campaign on behalf of (or in opposition to) any candidate for elective public office."

The so-called Johnson Amendment passed Con- gress without debate and was signed into law as part of the 1954 Internal Revenue Code by President Dwight Eisenhower. The measure was uncontroversial at the

time and for most of its history; it carried over into
the Internal Revenue Code of 1986, enacted during the
Reagan administration, which actually strenghtened
the prohibition against the use of tax-exempt funds for
political purposes.

Leaders of the Religious Right in recent years, however, have been pushing for a repeal of the Johnson
Amendment. They argue that pastors should be able to
make political endorsements from the pulpit without
jeopardizing their churches' tax exemptions. The fact
that they cannot now do so, they argue, represents an
infringement on their religious freedom and freedom
of speech, both protected by the First Amendment.

That is, to put it mildly, a strained interpretation. The
Johnson Amendment merely assures that taxpayers do
not subsidize partisan politicking. It also ensures that
tax-exempt organizations do not serve as the conduit
for tax-exempt contributions to political candidates, a
provision even more important in an age when "dark
money" — unaccounted cash — is constantly flowing
into campaign coffers. Do churches and other nonprofit
organizations really want to be complicit in further
undermining the integrity of the electoral process?

By complaining about the supposed limitations on
their freedom of speech, these leaders of the Religious
Right fail to acknowledge that tax exemption is a form

of public subsidy. The vast majority of the nation's religious organizations — churches, temples, mosques, synagogues — pay no taxes (other than Social Security taxes on wages), no income or corporate tax, and, in particular, no property taxes, although some organizations make voluntary contributions to their communities.

We can have a vigorous conversation about whether such an exemption is a good thing. (I think, on balance, it is; the founders recognized the value of voluntary associations and sought to encourage them.) But that discussion aside, the bottom line is that taxpayers in any given community effectively subsidize religious groups by paying extra taxes to support municipal services such as police protection, firefighters, parks, snow removal, road maintenance, and the like.

These institutions certainly benefit from those services. If a fire breaks out, for example, the fire department responds — even though these religious organizations pay no property taxes to support that service. Local taxpayers pay instead, taking up the slack for the tax exemption on property that otherwise might be valued very highly. (In addition, ordained ministers receive government subsidy on their personal taxes with a "fair rental value," which allows them to deduct housing expenses from their clergy income.)

To state it plainly, tax exemption is a form of public subsidy. All the Johnson Amendment requires is that, in exchange for that subsidy, the beneficiaries refrain from partisan politicking.

For decades, until very recently, churches and other tax-exempt organizations have regarded this as a pretty good trade-off: We'll accept public subsidies (in the form of not paying taxes) in exchange for refraining from political endorsements. For several years now, however, many leaders of the Religious Right have chafed under those restrictions. Various entities, including the Alliance Defending Freedom, have urged pastors to defy the law and endorse political candidates. Jay Sekulow, former chief counsel for the American Center for Law and Justice and then attorney for Donald Trump, asserted that the Johnson Amendment "prevents religious leaders from truly exercising their constitutionally-protected free speech rights when they act in their official capacity as a pastor or head of a religious, tax-exempt organization."

Let's be clear: Pastors, churches, or any other religious entity can make political endorsements from the pulpit or in any other forum. They need only to renounce their tax exemptions — their public subsidies — and they are free to be as partisan as they wish.

But there is another reason why the Johnson Amendment is a good idea and should not be repealed. Religion has flourished in the United States as nowhere else in the world precisely because the government has stayed out of the realm of religion, and vice versa. Despite the Religious Right's persistent attempts to circumvent it, the First Amendment is the best friend that religion ever had. It ensures that there is no established church, no state religion, and that religious groups can compete for adherents on an equal footing. And evangelicals in particular, by the way, have historically fared very well in the free marketplace of religion established by the First Amendment.

One can certainly argue that the Johnson Amendment's origins were less than pristine. Lyndon Johnson, the master strategist, did not act out of altruistic or even patriotic motives; he sought to enhance his prospects for reelection. But that in no way diminishes the wisdom of the Johnson Amendment, which both derives from and builds upon the First Amendment. It reinforces the wall of separation between church and state that was advocated by Roger Williams, founder of the Baptist tradition in America, and was encoded into the First Amendment to the Constitution. And we should also remember that Williams wanted a "wall of separation" between the "garden of the church" and the "wilderness of the world" because he feared that the integrity of the faith would be compromised by entanglement with politics.

That's a lesson worth recalling today, especially when the establishment clause of the First Amendment is imperiled.

13

JOHN F. KENNEDY AND SCHOOL PRAYER

The young president was prepared for the question. Two days earlier, on June 25, 1962, the US Supreme Court had issued its decision in a landmark case, *Engel v. Vitale*, which held that prescribed prayer in public schools violated the establishment clause of the Constitution.

The state of New York had passed legislation that encouraged students to begin each school day with a recitation of the Pledge of Allegiance and what became known as the Regents Prayer: "Almighty God, we acknowledge our dependence upon Thee, and we beg Thy blessings upon us, our parents, our teachers and our country. Amen."

Although the law allowed students to exempt themselves from the prayer, a group of parents from Long Island, led by Lawrence Roth (though Steven I. Engel's name appeared first), filed suit, arguing that the reference to "Almighty God" contradicted their religious beliefs and represented a violation of the establishment clause of the First Amendment. The plaintiffs, supported by the American Civil Liberties Union, were identified as two Jews, a Unitarian, an atheist, and a member of the New York Society for Ethical Culture. The court of appeals for New York had upheld the constitutionality of the prayer, and twenty-two states filed amicus briefs supporting the prayer. The American Ethical Union, the American Jewish Committee, and the Synagogue Council of America urged the court to find the prayer unconstitutional.

In a 6 to 1 decision, the Supreme Court agreed that the prayer was a prescribed religious activity and therefore violated the establishment clause of the First Amendment. As Hugo Black wrote in his majority opinion, "It is no part of the business of government to compose official prayers for any group of the American people to recite as a part of a religious program carried on by government."

Public reaction to the decision was overwhelmingly negative; a majority of Americans — 85 percent, according to a Gallup poll — objected to the ruling. The plaintiffs received angry phone calls and threats of violence. Many people expressed the concern that the Supreme Court's decision had "kicked God out of the schools." As one letter to the editor declared, "Almighty God has been given his walking papers," and George C. Wallace, the segregationist governor of Alabama, denounced the decision as "the bitter fruit of the liberal dogma that worships human intelligence and scorns the concept of divinity." A member of Congress from Alabama directed his anger at the justices. "They put the Negroes in the schools," he said, referring to the court's 1954 *Brown v. Board of Education* decision, "now they put God out of the schools." The John Birch Society stepped up its campaign to impeach Earl Warren, the chief justice, with billboards screaming SAVE PRAYER and SAVE AMERICA. One protester unfurled a banner that read, IMPEACH THE PRO-RED SUPREME COURT.

John F. Kennedy, the nation's first Roman Catholic president, was in a dicey situation. In 1949, Beacon Press had published *American Freedom and Catholic Power*, by Paul Blanshard, whose educational pedigree included the University of Michigan, Columbia and Harvard universities, and Union Theological Seminary. "I believe that every American — Catholic and non-Catholic — has a duty to speak on the Catholic question," Blanshard wrote, "because the issues involved go to the heart of our culture and our citizenship." Blanshard warned against the pernicious influence of the Roman Catholic hierarchy, adding that the church "uses the political power of some twenty-six million official American Catholics to bring American foreign policy into line with Vatican temporal interests." *American Freedom and Catholic Power* went through eleven printings in as many months, and as Kennedy set his eyes on the presidency during the 1950s, he understood that he would have to contend with a lingering anti-Catholicism in American life.

The so-called religious issue bedeviled Kennedy's campaign for the presidency in 1960; despite his promise not to raise the issue, Billy Graham colluded with other Protestant leaders to undermine Kennedy, and thereby boost Richard Nixon, in the general election. A closed-door gathering of 150 Protestant ministers — all or most of them already Nixon supporters — at the Mayflower Hotel in Washington, DC, on September 7, 1960, finally persuaded Kennedy that he needed to confront the religious issue directly.

Kennedy's address to the Greater Houston Ministerial Association, at the Rice Hotel on September 12, 1960, remains a classic statement about the relationship between church and state, particularly as it relates to a candidate's faith. Kennedy affirmed the separation of church and state as enshrined in the First Amendment and reminded his auditors that the harassment of Baptist preachers in Virginia had led to Thomas Jefferson's statute of religious freedom. Kennedy pointedly remarked that he was not the Catholic candidate for president; he was "the Democratic Party's nominee for president who happens also to be a Catholic."

Kennedy's audience that evening was respectful but wary; not once was the speech interrupted by applause. His appeal to religious freedom, his refusal to support an American ambassador to the Vatican, and the reiteration of his opposition to taxpayer support for parochial or any religious schools reassured enough Americans that he was able to win the presidency, albeit by a slim margin.

Still, despite the president's tepid piety, many Protestants remained skeptical of a Catholic in the White House. The Supreme Court's decision in *Engel v. Vitale* did little to assuage their concerns that Protestant hegemony in the United States was slipping away.

Kennedy's response to a question about the ruling opened with a generic statement about the importance of respect for the law, including Supreme Court decisions "even when we may not agree with them." He continued with a remark that struck at the heart of the matter: The Supreme Court did not outlaw prayer; it outlawed prescribed prayer in a public setting. We have an easy remedy, the president said, "and that is to pray ourselves." He continued, "And I would think that it would be a welcome reminder to every American family that we can pray a good deal more at home, we can attend our churches with a good deal more fidelity, and we can make the true meaning of prayer much more important in the lives of all of our children. That power is very much open to us."

A year later, the Supreme Court issued a complementary ruling in *Abington School District v. Schempp*, which outlawed school-sponsored Bible reading in the public schools. This was not the first time courts had ruled on the matter. During the so-called Cincinnati Bible War in 1869, when the school board rescinded prayer and Bible reading in an effort to attract more Catholic children into the public schools, conservative Protestants had sought an injunction to stop the rescission. Although the local superior court sided with the plaintiffs, Alphonso Taft, a judge and father to the future president and chief justice, disagreed. Allowing Protestants "to have their mode of worship and their bible used in the common schools," Taft argued, "is to hold to the union of Church and State." The Ohio Supreme Court unanimously agreed, ruling that religion lies "outside the true and legitimate province of government."

In the wake of the *Abington* decision of 1963, as with the earlier *Engel* ruling, many Americans once again responded with outrage. "God and religion have all but been driven from the public schools," the *Washington Evening Star* lamented. Wallace of Alabama was defiant. "I don't care what they say in Washington," the governor declared, "we are going to keep right on praying and reading the Bible in the public schools of Alabama." Billy Graham declared the decision wrong and adopted a majoritarian argument. "Eighty percent of the American people want Bible reading and prayer in the schools," he said. "Why should a majority be so severely penalized by the protests of a handful?"

Kennedy's statement following the *Engel* decision applies equally to the *Abington* ruling. The Supreme Court did not outlaw Bible reading in public schools any more than it outlawed prayer in public schools. Students, on their own, can do both. The Supreme Court merely decided, in deference to the establishment clause of the First Amendment, that the state cannot mandate such activities. As a federal court ruled in rejecting a challenge to a school district that had, in accordance with the *Engel* decision, forbidden public prayer, "The plaintiffs must content themselves with having their children say these prayers before 9 A.M. and after 3 P.M."

14

"SOUL LIBERTY," ROY'S ROCK, AND THE NEED FOR MORE BAPTISTS

America needs more Baptists. Real, traditional Baptists.

This point was brought resoundingly and hilariously to life for me when my mentor from college sent me a link to a 2015 meeting of the Okaloosa County School Board in Florida. As nearly as I can determine, some members of the community sought to open the board meetings with prayer. The school board attorney counseled against it, citing a small technicality called the First Amendment to the Constitution and its proscription against religious establishment. Undeterred, the pious Christians of Okaloosa County decided that public prayer could be offered before the school board meeting was gaveled to order.

The stage was set. One citizen opened this revival/board meeting by quoting verses of scripture: Matthew 6:24 (no one can serve two masters), Galatians 2:20 (crucified with Christ), Matthew 22:37 (love God with all your heart, soul, and mind), Ephesians 4:27 (give no opportunity to the devil), and Matthew 4:10 (worship the Lord your God).

Had the reader quoted Matthew 6:6 — "But when you pray, go into your room, close the door and pray to your Father, who is unseen. Then your Father, who sees what is done in secret, will reward you" — the ensuing donnybrook might have been averted.

After the scripture recitations, the man turned the meeting over to several pastors to lead the prayers (apparently religion is a tag-team sport in Okaloosa County), who were greeted with applause. As the first pastor started praying, "Father God, we just come before you . . . ," a middle-aged man began his prayer: "Mother, Father God of all peoples, we come today in our humble way to shape a small part of your creation." He proceeded to invoke every deity imaginable, from Yahweh and Dionysus and Isis to Krishna, Ekankar, and Buddha. "May we be imbued by the wisdom of all gods," he continued.

The good Christian folks of Okaloosa County were not amused. If there was to be prayer in advance of the school board meeting, it would be Christian prayer, dammit. The majority of folks in Okaloosa County, after all, are Christians.

After their initial shock at this interloper's effrontery, the good citizens of Okaloosa County tried to shout him down, offering their prayers more loudly and insistently, arms raised. Some were speaking in tongues.

Soon the school board meeting sounded like a cacophony, each voice seeking to drown out the others.

The lone dissenter persisted, at one point sitting in the lotus position in an apparent attempt to meditate. He invited someone nearby to join him, but the citizens of Okaloosa County by then had segued into congregational singing: "Amazing Grace," "What a Friend We Have in Jesus," "Nothing But the Blood of Jesus."

Mayhem. Utter mayhem. The clip closes with one of the citizens shouting over and over, "In the name of Jesus! In the name of Jesus!" He tried to perform an exorcism on the poor, misguided soul who dared to offer prayers to a deity other than one approved by the majority. "We cast you out in Jesus' name," the exorcist shouted, although it wasn't clear if he was casting out the demon or the interloper.

What does all this have to do with Baptists? Roger Williams, founder of the Baptist tradition in America, believed in religious toleration and liberty of conscience. Having been persecuted and banished from Massachusetts for his religious convictions, Williams determined that Rhode Island would be a haven of toleration. He also warned that too close an association between church and state would be detrimental to the integrity of the faith, that the "wilderness of the world" would encroach on the "garden of the church."

Other Baptists throughout American history have upheld that tradition. Isaac Backus was converted during the Great Awakening, became a preacher several years later, and organized a group of "Separate Baptists" in Middleborough, Massachusetts, in 1756. Resenting the fact that taxes in Massachusetts supported Congregationalist ministers, Backus published *An Appeal to the Public for Religious Liberty, Against the Oppressions of the Present Day* in 1773. Several years later, he proposed language for the Massachusetts Constitution that would guarantee that "every person has an inalienable right to act in all religious affairs according to the full persuasion of his own mind, where others are not injured thereby."

The Baptist tradition of "soul liberty" continued into the twentieth century. On a Sunday afternoon, May 16, 1920, George Washington Truett, pastor of First Baptist Church in Dallas, Texas, walked to the lectern set up for him on the east steps of the Capitol in Washington, DC. Addressing a massive crowd of ten to fifteen thousand, Truett opened with a paean to the United States and declared that "the supreme contribution of the new world to the old is the contribution of religious liberty." Indeed, it was "the chiefest contribution that America has thus far made to civilization," and Truett was proud to announce to his audience that the separation of church and state was "pre-eminently a Baptist achievement."

Truett continued with a ringing endorsement of Baptist principles, especially civil and religious liberty. Baptists affirmed, he said, "the natural and fundamental and indefeasible right of every human being to worship God or not, according to the dictates of his conscience, and, as long as he does not infringe upon the rights of others, he is to be held accountable alone to God for all religious beliefs and practices." This principle extends beyond mere toleration to absolute liberty: "Toleration is a concession, while liberty is a right."

Like Williams and Backus before him, Truett insisted that faith should be voluntary. "It is the consistent and insistent contention of our Baptist people, always and everywhere, that religion must be forever voluntary and uncoerced, and that it is not the prerogative of any power, whether civil or ecclesiastical, to compel men to conform to any religious creed or form of worship," he thundered. "God wants free worshipers and no other kind."

According to Truett, Baptists recognized that enjoying religious liberty for themselves entailed defending it for others. "A Baptist would rise at midnight to plead for absolute religious liberty," he declared, "for his Catholic neighbor, and for his Jewish neighbor, and for every-

body else." And in a final salvo that might have antic-
ipated the chicanery of Roy Moore, chief justice of the
Alabama Supreme Court, seven decades later, Truett
declared, "Christ's religion needs no prop of any kind
from any worldly source, and to the degree that it is
thus supported is a millstone hanged about its neck."

Because Baptists were once a minority themselves,
they eschewed majoritarianism, the notion that what-
ever faith or ideology claims the allegiance of a majority
should prevail. Roger Williams and Isaac Backus were
representatives of religious minorities who looked to the
government for protection from the entrenched, established majority. Their putative descendants, however,
seek to impose their religious views on all Americans,
thereby violating not only the First Amendment but the
very principles that define their own religious heritage.

All of these — liberty of conscience ("soul liberty"),
separation of church and state, respect for the rights
of minorities — were bedrock Baptist principles, jeal-
ously guarded by generations of Baptists . . . until 1979.
With the conservative takeover of the Southern Baptist
Convention in June 1979, the largest Protestant denomination in the United States abandoned its historic role
as watchman on the wall of separation between church
and state. The denomination's new leaders, adopting a
majoritarian ethic, began to silence dissenting voices

— on doctrinal matters, especially the ordination of women — but on political issues as well. Working hand in hand with the newly emergent Religious Right, these folks who called themselves Baptists began to level the wall of separation between church and state, calling for state support of religious schools, the enactment of legislation narrowly informed by religious interests, and the display of religious symbols in public spaces.

W. A. Criswell, longtime pastor of First Baptist Church in Dallas, and sometime president of the Southern Baptist Convention, illustrates this shift. When John F. Kennedy was running for president in 1960, Criswell declared, "It is written in our country's constitution that church and state must be, in this nation, forever separate and free." All expressions of faith, he added, must be voluntary, and "in the very nature of the case, there can be no proper union of church and state." During the Reagan era, however, the heyday of the Religious Right, Criswell changed his tune: "I believe this notion of the separation of church and state was the figment of some infidel's imagination."

I suspect that many of the citizens attending the school board melee in Okaloosa County would call themselves Baptists; they live in a region of the country where, as Bill Moyers once remarked, there are more Baptists than people. But they are not real Baptists. A real Baptist true to her convictions honors and defends the separation of church and state. A real Baptist, part of a tradition that was once a persecuted minority, abhors majoritarianism and upholds liberty of conscience. A real Baptist, following Roger Williams, recognizes that when faith and politics are conflated, it is the faith that suffers. It becomes trivialized and fetishized.

Roy Stewart Moore attended the United States Military Academy at West Point, where he graduated in 1969. After service as a military policeman in Vietnam — where he was known, not affectionately, as "Captain America" for his zeal — Moore returned to Alabama and earned his law degree in 1977 from the University of Alabama. After a stint as a deputy district attorney in Etowah County, he ran for a circuit court judgeship and was defeated badly. He headed then for Texas to embark on a career as a professional kickboxer and then to the outback of Australia. He returned to Alabama in 1984 and briefly set up private practice in Gadsden. Moore was then appointed to fill a vacant circuit court judgeship in Gadsden; he ran and won election to the bench in his own right in 1992.

Moore opened his court sessions with prayer and hung a hand-carved wooden plaque depicting the Ten Commandments in his courtroom, an action that, his

critics said, represented an infringement of the establishment clause of the First Amendment. The American
Civil Liberties Union filed suit in 1995 to have the plaque
removed. The people of Alabama, however, rather than
censure his flouting of the Constitution, rewarded
Moore by electing him chief justice of the Alabama
Supreme Court in 2000; Moore, running as a Republican, had campaigned for office as the "Ten Commandments Judge."

Shortly after his election, he commissioned a local
gravestone company to produce a monument emblazoned with the Decalogue. Late in the evening of July
31, 2001, Moore and a work crew, laboring through
the night, installed the two-and-one-half-ton granite
monument, which would come to be known as "Roy's
Rock," in the lobby of the Alabama Judicial Building in
Montgomery.

As it happens, I was one of the expert witnesses in
the so-called Ten Commandments case in Alabama.
My testimony was that the First Amendment and the
separation of church and state was the best thing that
ever happened to religion in the United States. We have
a salubrious religious culture here in America, one
unmatched anywhere in the world, and it is precisely
because of the First Amendment, which allows religion
to flourish. As Roger Williams warned long ago, any

attempt to blur the line of separation diminishes the integrity of the faith.

Judge Myron Thompson ruled — correctly — that "Roy's Rock" violated the First Amendment and must be removed. As the workers were preparing to relocate the monument, one of the protesters screamed, "Get your hands off my God!"

Unless I miss my guess, one of the commandments etched into the side of that monument said something about graven images. And that was precisely Roger Williams's point about protecting the faith from trivialization by too close an association with politics and the state. And I suspect Williams would also have something to say to those believers screeching their piety at a school board meeting in Florida.

"Baptists have one consistent record concerning liberty throughout their long and eventful history," George Washington Truett declared from the steps of the Capitol in 1920. "They have never been a party to oppression of conscience."

America needs more Baptists.

15

THE BATTLE CRY OF "RELIGIOUS FREEDOM"

The emergence of the Religious Right in the mid-1970s provided American evangelicals with a new vocabulary for talking about religious freedom and, in many ways, upended their prior approaches to the relationship between church and state. During the controversy over public prayer in public schools in the 1960s, for example, evangelicals employed majoritarian arguments: Because the majority of Americans were Christians, a Christian prayer was therefore appropriate. As Edgar Koons, a pastor in Sacramento, California, put it, "The great majority favors God." Evangelicals, however, began to reverse field in the 1970s, adopting the posture of embattled minority, a strategy that evangelicals have since employed in arguments over same-sex marriage and medical coverage for contraception.

The political movement that became known as the Religious Right mobilized not, as commonly supposed, to battle abortion, but rather to defend racial segregation in evangelical institutions such as Bob Jones University. In May 1969 a group of parents in Holmes

County, Mississippi, noting that the number of white students in the public schools had dropped to zero by the second year of desegregation, filed suit to block the granting of tax-exempt status to three "segregation academies," schools founded to evade desegregation of the public schools, a process set in motion by the Supreme Court's landmark *Brown v. Board of Education* ruling of 1954 and fortified by the Civil Rights Act a decade later. That suit was joined with another suit and eventually reached the district court of the District of Columbia in a case called *Green v. Connally*. On June 30, 1971, the court decided for the plaintiffs, ruling that any institution that engages in racial discrimination is *by definition* not a charitable institution and therefore has no claims on tax-exempt status.

As the Internal Revenue Service proceeded to enforce that ruling in the 1970s, evangelical leaders like Jerry Falwell, who had his own segregation academy in Lynchburg, Virginia, began to mobilize politically. For nearly two decades, conservative activist Paul Weyrich, the architect of the Religious Right, had tried various issues to pique evangelical interest in politics, including pornography, school prayer, the proposed Equal Rights Amendment to the Constitution, and abortion. When "the Internal Revenue Service tried to deny tax exemption to private schools," Weyrich said in a 1980 interview with *Conservative Digest*, that "more than any single act brought the fundamentalists and evangelicals into the political process." He reiterated the point about evangelicals a decade later. "I was trying to get these people interested in those issues and I utterly failed," Weyrich recalled in 1990. "What changed their mind was Jimmy Carter's intervention against the Christian schools, trying to deny them tax-exempt status on the basis of so-called de facto segregation."

Weyrich, along with other Republican operatives, including Paul Pressler, Ed McAteer, and others, targeted Southern and Independent Baptists as the new base for the party. Weyrich also encouraged Robert Billings, an evangelical, to form an organization called Christian School Action as a vehicle for building on evangelical discontent, an organization Weyrich came to regard as a "tremendous asset" to his hopes for politicizing conservative evangelicals. Billings, who had earlier founded the National Christian Action Coalition to thwart what he characterized as "an attempt by the IRS to control private schools," quickly mobilized evangelical ministers. Billings later declared that Jerome Kurtz, head of the Internal Revenue Service, "has done more to bring Christians together than any man since the Apostle Paul." Even Anita Bryant, who had been goaded into activism by her opposition to gay rights, recognized the centrality of the school issue. "I believe the day of the comfortable Christian is over," Bryant declared. "Maybe it hasn't reached everybody in the rural areas, but it's a battle in the cities to keep them from taking over and reaching private and religious schools."

In ramping up for political activism, evangelicals portrayed themselves as defending what they considered the sanctity of the evangelical subculture from outside interference. Weyrich astutely picked up on those fears. "What caused the movement to surface was the federal government's moves against Christian schools," Weyrich reiterated in 1990. "This absolutely shattered the Christian community's notions that Christians could isolate themselves inside their own institutions and teach what they pleased." For agitated evangelicals, Weyrich's conservative gospel of less government suddenly struck a responsive chord. "It wasn't the abortion issue; that wasn't sufficient," Weyrich recalled. "It was the recognition that isolation simply would no longer work in this society."

Weyrich's genius lay in his ability to shift the terms of debate from a defense of racial discrimination in evangelical institutions to a supposed defense of religious liberty, all the while conveniently ignoring the fact that tax exemption is a form of public subsidy. Suddenly, evangelicalism, arguably the most influential social and religious movement in American history, adopted the posture of a persecuted minority. All protestations about a "moral majority" notwithstanding, leaders of the Religious Right began to argue that their institutions were under assault by a "secular majority."

This rhetoric of victimization has fueled the Religious Right ever since the late 1970s. Ironically, it helped to elect Ronald Reagan over Jimmy Carter, an evangelical, in 1980, and it has been used ever since to summon the faithful to the political ramparts. It's our religious freedom that is under assault, they assert; we're the embattled minority struggling for survival. "From the Senate chamber to a corner bakery," the Family Research Council complained, "Christians with natural or biblical views of marriage and sexuality have a bullseye on their backs."

No one articulated this more clearly than Bob Jones III, president of Bob Jones University, after the Supreme Court ruled in 1983 that the school could no longer retain both its racially exclusionary policies and its tax exemption. "We're in a bad fix in America when eight evil old men and one vain and foolish woman can speak a verdict on American liberties," Jones complained. "Our nation from this day forward is no better than Russia insofar as expecting the blessings of God is concerned. You no longer live in a nation that is religiously free."

Religious freedom, for Jones and his university, meant freedom to discriminate — at taxpayer expense.

More recently, this argument has been used by religious conservatives to deny business services to same-sex couples (*Masterpiece Cakeshop v. Colorado Civil Rights Commission*) and to deny health insurance coverage for contraception (*Burwell v. Hobby Lobby*). Claiming the mantle of victim and marching under the banner of religious liberty, the Religious Right has cleverly reversed field, abandoning majoritarianism in favor of the rhetoric of victimization — and, in so doing, have found a sympathetic audience in an increasingly conservative Supreme Court.

16

THE CASE AGAINST CHRISTIAN NATIONALISM

The sight of a politician hawking Bibles — whether in Lafayette Square or in an infomercial — is more than a bit unsettling, especially when that politician has little sense about what the Bible contains. And when the Bible comes bundled with the Constitution, the Declaration of Independence, and the Pledge of Allegiance, as was the case with the *God Bless the USA Bible* that Donald Trump promoted for $59.99 while a presidential candidate in 2024, you can bet something more is at stake.

"Religion and Christianity are the two biggest things missing from this country," Trump declared — this coming from a self-confessed sexual predator and someone who, according to independent sources, issued more than thirty thousand false or misleading statements during his first four years in office.

Despite — or perhaps because of — the messenger, the message of Christian nationalism has been amplified in recent years, although this is nothing new in American history. At various moments, in perceived times of crisis, Christians have pushed to designate the United States as a Christian nation, despite the First Amendment's explicit disavowal of religious establishment.

During the War of 1812, for instance, Timothy Dwight, president of Yale, bemoaned the absence of references to God and Christianity in the nation's charter documents. One of the Confederacy's criticisms of the Union was the lack of Christian language in the Constitution, so the South took pains to declare that the Confederate States of America was a Christian enterprise. This in turn prompted the formation of a group calling itself the National Reform Association to propose a constitutional amendment designating the United States as a Christian nation, crediting "the Lord Jesus Christ as the Ruler among the nations."

When presented with this proposal, Abraham Lincoln wisely temporized, averring that "the work of amending the Constitution should not be done hastily." But that hasn't stopped other efforts to amend the Constitution in ways that would run contrary to the First Amendment. The National Reform Association is still active, still pushing for changes to the Constitution, but more recent attempts to anoint the United States as a Christian nation have steered clear of proposed amendments and focused instead on two strategies.

The first is a series of incremental measures to subvert the First Amendment, both by legislation and by judicial rulings. Especially in states like Iowa, Texas, Florida, and Oklahoma, Republican governors and supermajorities in the statehouse have crafted laws that divert taxpayer money to religious schools. The US Supreme Court, with its right-wing majority's scant regard for the First Amendment, has been steadily whittling away at the establishment clause, notably in its *Espinoza v. Montana* and *Carson v. Makin* decisions, which ruled that government-funded scholarships and vouchers for students attending private schools could not exclude religious schools.

The second recent strategy for the advance of Christian nationalism is positively Trumpian: Simply declare that, all evidence to the contrary notwithstanding, the United States is and always has been a Christian nation. The driving force behind this campaign of prevarication is David Barton, a faux historian who has crafted an entire career out of asserting that the founders were evangelical Christians and that the nation was explicitly founded on Christian principles.

Barton's "history" has been discredited, especially and most thoroughly by Warren Throckmorton, emeritus professor at Grove City College in Pennsylvania. Barton habitually wrenches quotations out of context or fabricates quotations out of whole cloth, malpractice so egregious that his very conservative publisher, Thomas Nelson, withdrew Barton's book *The Jefferson Lies* from publication in 2012. That has not deterred Barton or his right-wing acolytes from propagating falsehoods in pursuit of Christian nationalism. So let's review, once again, the historical record.

The founders, well aware of the wars of religion in Europe and England, explicitly specified that the new government should have no entanglement with religion. The First Amendment is abundantly clear: "Congress shall make no law respecting an establishment of religion, or prohibiting the free exercise thereof."

Christian nationalists like to make a big case out of the fact that the phrase *separation of church and state* appears nowhere in the Constitution. That is certainly true, but any plain reading of the text, two hundred years ago or today, reveals that this is precisely what the founders intended. Certainly Thomas Jefferson understood the meaning. On January 1, 1802, responding to a letter from the Baptists of Danbury, Connecticut, the third president quoted a portion of the First Amendment together with his interpretation: "I contemplate with sovereign reverence that act of the whole American people which declared that their legislature should 'make no law respecting an establishment of religion, or prohibiting the free exercise thereof,' thus building a wall of separation between Church & State."

The argument for Christian nationalism, therefore, that the United States is and always has been a Christian nation, falters on legal grounds. The First Amendment, America's best idea, prohibits the establishment of any religion, and when Patrick Henry introduced a bill designating Christianity as the favored religion in Virginia, James Madison led the charge against it, and the legislation was defeated.

Barton and his right-wing compatriots also like to assert that the founders themselves were evangelical Christians. This is so ludicrous that I'm tempted not to dignify it with a response. Many of the founders were deists, who understood God as a remote and disinterested entity. John Adams recoiled at the notion of Jesus as incarnate deity, which he thought was "the Source of almost all the Corruptions of Christianity." Jefferson himself excised references to Jesus' divinity and miracles from the New Testament; this expurgated version, published posthumously, has come to be known as the Jefferson Bible.

Jefferson expressed his fondest hope that Americans would eventually embrace the "rational Christianity" of Unitarians, those who believe that Jesus was a moral exemplar but not the son of God. "I trust that there is not a young man now living in the U.S.," he wrote, "who will not die an Unitarian." Indeed, no founder, with the possible exceptions of John Witherspoon, Presbyterian minister and president of the College of New Jersey, and Benjamin Rush, a physician, would qualify for membership in any of the churches now advocating for Christian nationalism.

Finally, the Treaty of Tripoli was negotiated during the George Washington administration, sent to Congress by then president John Adams with his endorsement, and ratified unanimously by the US Senate on June 7, 1797. Article 11 of the treaty reads in part, "The government of the United States of America is not in any sense founded on the Christian religion."

Aside from the prevarications and the misrepresentations on the part of Christian nationalists, the huge irony here is that the First Amendment's mandate to separate church and state is the best thing that ever happened to religion in America. The disestablishment and free exercise clauses set up a free marketplace for religion in the United States, where no one faith enjoys the sanction of the state. This marketplace, as Adam Smith had predicted in his 1776 brief for free-market capitalism, *The Wealth of Nations*, has allowed religious entrepreneurs to compete for popular followings, thereby ensuring a competitive, populist religious marketplace.

Evangelicals, who know almost instinctively how to speak the idiom of the culture, have flourished in this marketplace. Untethered by tradition, creeds, liturgy, or hierarchy, they have nimbly adapted to social changes, from the open-air preaching of George Whitefield and other itinerants in the eighteenth century and the circuit riders and camp meetings of the nineteenth century to the urban revivalism of Billy Sunday and Billy Graham in the twentieth century and the suburban, shopping-mall-style megachurches of more recent vintage.

No group has benefited more from the First Amendment than evangelicals, the very cohort that is now trying to breach the wall of separation between church and state in the name of Christian nationalism. And therein lies danger: too close an association between church and state.

The person who saw this danger most clearly was Roger Williams, founder of the Baptist tradition in America. Williams, a Puritan and graduate of Cambridge University, migrated to Massachusetts in 1631, but he soon ran afoul of the Puritan authorities because of his criticism of Puritan theocracy, which sought to merge church and state. In 1635, Williams was convicted of "diverse, new, and dangerous opinions" and banished from Massachusetts. He fled on foot to what is now Rhode Island, purchased land from the Narragansetts, and eventually

established a colony that would ensure religious freedom and liberty of conscience. "I desired it might be a
shelter for persons distressed for conscience," Williams
declared.

In 1644, Williams argued for separating the "garden of
the church" from the "wilderness of the world" by means
of a "wall of separation." That metaphor has become so
familiar that we sometimes lose sight of its importance.
And to understand it fully we need to remember that
people in the seventeenth century were not members
of the Sierra Club — that is to say, they did not share
our romantic, post-Thoreauvian notions about wilderness. For them, wilderness was a place of danger where
evil lurked. So when Williams talked about shielding
the "garden of the church" from the "wilderness of the
world," his concern was protecting the faith from too
close an association with the state, a lesson that Christian nationalists would do well to recall.

For people who claim the Bible as their sole authority
— and who seek, many of them, to translate what they
call "biblical principles" into the civil and criminal law
— the New Testament itself provides ample refutation
to any scheme of Christian nationalism. Jesus himself,
according to the Gospel of John, declared, "My kingdom is not of this world," and St. Paul instructed the
early believers to be subordinate to civil authorities.

So if Christian nationalism has no theological under-pinning and no warrant in American history, what is the appeal? Why would so many white evangelicals respond to the demonstrably false statements of David Barton or covet a *God Bless the USA Bible* that bundles the King James Version with the Pledge of Allegiance and the nation's charter documents?

As in times past, the impetus to push for Christian nationalism occurs in times of perceived crisis: the War of 1812, the Civil War, the Cold War. White evangeli-cals asserting the Christian origins of the United States have been told by their leaders that they are under siege, that their values are no longer ascendant in a multicul-tural American society. There's a smidgeon of truth to that, I suppose, although evangelicals have wielded extraordinary political influence since the late 1970s and continue to do so. But the rhetoric of victimization, especially when combined with nostalgia for a supposed halcyon past, is catnip to white evangelicals, and one of the attractions of Donald Trump is that he speaks the language of victimization better than anyone I've seen. It's always about him, of course; he's the victim. But evangelicals recognize that vocabulary because the genius of the Religious Right is that its leaders have always portrayed themselves — and by extension, all evangelicals — as marginal and as victims.

The supposed remedy is the assertion that the United States is and always has been a Christian nation, with the corollary that anyone who falls outside that designation — immigrants, minorities, those who cannot claim conventional sexual identities — are aliens, entitled at best to second-class status.

Nothing could be more at odds with the nation's charter documents, which are notable for their protection of minorities. The founders, for all their faults — slaveholding being the most egregious — never intended the United States to be a majoritarian society. They allowed, even cherished, dissent. And throughout our history, sooner or later, we Americans have eventually risen to our better selves — far too slowly in the case of women and people of color — and sought to live up to the standards articulated by the founders.

Although those ideals remain not fully realized, we affirm them nonetheless. I consider myself a patriot — not because I wave flags or wear hideous red caps, but because my sense of American history is that Americans still care about those principles and will eventually find a way to honor them.

We are not a majoritarian society, where the majority dictates to everyone else, and that is the fundamental flaw of Christian nationalism, whose advocates seek to encode what they consider "Christian" principles.

The First Amendment's proscription against religious establishment was a blow against majoritarianism and an assurance that all religious convictions (including no religion at all) would be guaranteed "free exercise." That's a far cry from asserting that the United States is and always has been a Christian nation.

The *God Bless the USA Bible* apparently includes the Bill of Rights. Those pushing for Christian nationalism might want to reacquaint themselves with the initial clause of the First Amendment: "Congress shall make no law respecting the establishment of religion or prohibiting the free exercise thereof."

AFTERWORD

The separation of church and state in America was an unprecedented experiment, but it was also born of necessity. Religious diversity was rife in the Atlantic colonies, with groups ranging from Catholics and Moravians to Jews, Quakers, and Dutch Reformed — and perhaps hundreds more. The founders' decision to forswear a religious establishment was a concession to that pluralism, and the example of the Middle Colonies, especially New York, New Jersey, and Pennsylvania, demonstrated that representatives of many different faith groups could coexist in relative harmony with one another without the state taking on the responsibility of designating one as the established religion.

The First Amendment to the Constitution codified that arrangement while simultaneously guaranteeing freedom of religious expression. This configuration of church and state has served the nation well, but it's also fair to say that some of the characters who have contributed bricks to the wall of separation have been less than savory or their motives less than pure. Roger

Williams, founder of the Baptist tradition in America
and to whom we owe thanks for the wall of separation
metaphor, was clearly a divisive figure, not only for the
Puritans in Massachusetts, who expelled him from the
colony, but also to his compatriots in Rhode Island.
Nevertheless, he correctly pointed out the dangers to the
integrity of faith from too close an association with the
state. Thomas Jefferson, despite his brilliance, despite
his soaring rhetoric about liberty, kept other human
beings shackled in the bonds of slavery, appropriating
the sweat of their labor for his own enrichment. A deist
and a rationalist, Jefferson cared little about matters of
faith, yet his embrace of disestablishment shielded the
ship of state of the new nation from the churning seas
of religious factionalism.

In the nineteenth century, James G. Blaine would
probably be categorized as a nativist and an anti-
Catholic bigot, and yet his "Blaine amendments,"
adopted by many states, staked out the important principle that in deference to the establishment clause of the
First Amendment taxpayer funds should not support
sectarian education. Lyndon Johnson was not demonstrably pious, but his Johnson Amendment erected a
barrier separating religious and other not-for-profit
groups from partisan politicking. The plaintiffs in *Engel
v. Vitale* and *Abington v. Schempp* were secularists,

even atheists, and yet, despite the howling protests that greeted those decisions in the early 1960s, the effect of the rulings was to protect the faith from being fetishized and trivialized by compulsory demonstrations of piety.

Despite the Constitution's declared policy of neutrality in matters of religion, the sheer number of Christians, especially Protestant Christians, has inflected American society, making it the nation's default faith. Although the margin of Christians to other religions or no religion at all (the "nones") has slackened in recent years, Christianity, in its various species, retains a powerful hold. When Barack Obama in the course of the 2008 presidential campaign was accused of being a Muslim, he countered with proof of his long-standing membership in a Christian church rather than offering a full-throated defense of Muslim Americans. Both as a candidate and as president, Obama frequently expressed his support for religious freedom and diversity, but he was also sensitive to the possibility that running for national office perceived as a Muslim might have imperiled his electoral prospects. John McCain, during the same campaign, defended Obama from the charge that he was an "Arab" by insisting that his opponent was a decent "family man," as if there were an inherent distinction between the two. Rather than point out the obvious — that being an Arab or a Muslim would not in the least disqualify

Obama from being president — McCain defended his opponent as a family man.

The forty-fifth and forty-seventh president of the United States, who launched his political career by challenging the circumstances of Barack Obama's nativity, made a point of taking the oath of office as Donald *John* Trump, in apparent contrast with his predecessor, Barack *Hussein* Obama. (Later, as president, Trump infamously sought to ban Muslims from entering the United States, based solely on their religion.) If Americans would fully embrace the First Amendment, if we are faithful to the founders' intent, we should acknowledge that the default of Christianity has affected our perceptions of who is truly American.

Despite a somewhat checkered history, however, the separation of church and state in the United States, this unprecedented experiment in Western culture, has proved remarkably resilient over the decades, the centuries. The genius of the founders lay in their determination to avoid entangling the two entities, recognizing that each would function better untrammeled by the other. Although religious factionalism is one of the characteristics of American life, those divisions have rarely impeded the functions of government, and religion in fact has often contributed to the common good. The First Amendment set up a free market for religion in the

United States, where no one expression of faith enjoys the support or the preferment of the state and where religious entrepreneurs (to extend the economic metaphor) compete with one another for popular followings. This has lent an energy and dynamism to religious life in America, a vitality unmatched anywhere in the world. As Justice Sandra Day O'Connor wrote in her final opinion on church–state matters: "Those who would renegotiate the boundaries between church and state must answer a difficult question: Why would we trade a system that has served us so well for one that has served others so poorly?"

Indeed, in the face of such a salubrious religious culture in the United States, one might assume that faith leaders would be content with this circumstance — and many are. But powerful enemies have mobilized against the First Amendment in recent years. Leaders of the Religious Right in particular have sought to collapse the wall of separation between church and state by advocating taxpayer-funded vouchers for sectarian schools, by installing religious symbols in public spaces, and by agitating for repeal of the Johnson Amendment, which forbids tax-exempt organizations from engaging in partisan politics. Since its inception in the 1970s, the Religious Right has invoked the specious argument of "religious liberty" to justify discrimination, first to defend racial

segregation in evangelical institutions and more recently
to deny the rights of minorities. The efforts on the part of
the Religious Right to undermine the First Amendment
have been abetted by the Supreme Court, most notably
its *Espinoza v. Montana Department of Revenue* decision.

Not that long ago, Americans could look to Baptists to
patrol the wall of separation between church and state.
Roger Williams, progenitor of the Baptist tradition in
America, sought to protect the "garden of the church"
from the "wilderness of the world" by means of a "wall
of separation." But the Southern Baptist Convention, the
largest Baptist group (and the largest Protestant denomination) in the nation, has largely abandoned that role,
with some of its leaders actually leading the effort to
breech the wall of separation, thereby linking the Southern Baptist denomination and congregations to the
Republican base and voting bloc.

The First Amendment has survived various attempts
to subvert it over the years, including legislation that
would have designated the United States as a Christian
nation. Those who appreciate the beauty of the First
Amendment and the prescience of the founders in separating church and state must remain forever vigilant.

SELECTED BIBLIOGRAPHY

Alberta, Tim. *The Kingdom, the Power, and the Glory: American Evangelicals in an Age of Extremism.* New York: Harper, 2023.

Balmer, Randall. *A Perfect Babel of Confusion: Dutch Religion and English Culture in the Middle Colonies.* New York: Oxford University Press, 1989.

Balmer, Randall, Lee Groberg, and Mark Mabry. *First Freedom: The Fight for Religious Liberty.* American Fork, Utah: Covenant Communications, 2012.

Barry, John M. *Roger Williams and the Creation of the American Soul.* New York: Viking, 2012.

Bellah, Robert N. "Civil Religion in America." *Dædalus: Journal of the American Academy of Arts and Sciences* 96 (Winter 1967), 1–21.

Beneke, Chris, and Christopher S. Grenda, eds. *The First Prejudice: Religious Tolerance and Intolerance in Early America.* Philadelphia: University of Pennsylvania Press, 2011.

———, eds. *The Lively Experiment: Religious Toleration in America from Roger Williams to the Present.* Foreword by Jon Butler. Lanham, Md.: Rowman & Littlefield, 2015.

Blantz, Thomas E. "James Gillespie Blaine, His Family, and 'Romanism.'" *Catholic Historical Review* 94 (October 2008), 695–716.

Bonomi, Patricia U. *Under the Cope of Heaven: Religion, Society, and Politics in Colonial America.* New York: Oxford University Press, 1986.

Boyd, Gregory A. *The Myth of a Christian Nation: How the Quest for Political Power Is Destroying the Church.* Grand Rapids, Mich.: Zondervan, 2007.

Brown, C. A. "Elder John Leland and the Mammoth Cheshire Cheese." *Agricultural History* 18 (October 1944), 145–53.

Church, Forrest, ed. *The Separation of Church and State: Writings on a Fundamental Freedom by America's Founders.* Boston: Beacon Press, 2004.

———. *So Help Me God: The Founding Fathers and the First Great Battle Over Church and State.* New York: Mariner Books, 2008.

Corrigan, John, and Lynn S. Neal. *Religious Intolerance in America: A Documentary History.* Chapel Hill: University of North Carolina Press, 2010.

Curry, Thomas J. *The First Freedoms: Church and State in America to the Passage of the First Amendment.* New York: Oxford University Press, 1986.

Davidson, James D. "Why Churches Cannot Endorse or Oppose Political Candidates." *Review of Religious Research* 40 (September 1998), 16–34.

Dierenfield, Bruce J. *The Battle Over School Prayer: How* Engel v. Vitale *Changed America.* Lawrence: University Press of Kansas, 2007.

Drakeman, Donald L. *Church, State, and Original Intent.* Cambridge, UK: Cambridge University Press, 2010.

Einwechter, William O., ed. *Explicitly Christian Politics: The Vision of the National Reform Association.* Pittsburgh: Christian Statesman Press, 1997.

Fea, John. *Was America Founded as a Christian Nation? A Historical Introduction.* Louisville, Ky.: Westminster John Knox Press, 2011.

Fessenden, Tracy. "The Nineteenth-Century Bible Wars and the Separation of Church and State." *Church History* 74 (December 2005), 784–811.

Garrison, Becky. *Roger Williams's Little Book of Virtues.* Eugene, Ore.: Wipf & Stock, 2020.

Gaustad, Edwin S. *Church and State in America.* 2nd ed. New York: Oxford University Press, 2003.

———. *Faith of the Founders: Religion and the New Nation, 1776–1826.* Foreword by Randall Balmer. Waco, Tex.: Baylor University Press, 2011.

———. *Liberty of Conscience: Roger Williams in America.* Grand Rapids, Mich.: Wm. B. Eerdmans, 1991.

Gordon, Sarah Barringer. *The Spirit of the Law: Religious Voices and the Constitution in Modern America*. Cambridge, Mass.: Harvard University Press, 2010.

Gordon-McCutchan, R. C. *The Taos Indians and the Battle for Blue Lake*. Santa Fe: Red Crane Books, 1991.

Green, Steven K. *The Bible, the School, and the Constitution: The Clash That Shaped Modern Church-State Doctrine*. New York: Oxford University Press, 2012.

———. *Inventing a Christian America: The Myth of the Religious Founding*. New York: Oxford University Press, 2015.

———. *The Second Disestablishment: Church and State in Nineteenth-Century America*. New York: Oxford University Press, 2010.

———. *The Third Disestablishment: Church, State, and American Culture, 1940–1975*. New York: Oxford University Press, 2019.

Greenawalt, Kent. "History as Ideology: Philip Hamburger's *Separation of Church and State*." *California Law Review* 93 (January 2005), 367–96.

Gorski, Phillip S., and Samuel L. Perry. *The Flag and the Cross: White Christian Nationalism and the Threat to American Democracy*. New York: Oxford University Press, 2022.

Goldberg, Michelle. *Kingdom Coming: The Rise of Christian Nationalism*. New York: W. W. Norton, 2007.

Haefeli, Evan. *New Netherland and the Dutch Origins of American Religious Liberty*. Philadelphia: University of Pennsylvania Press, 2012.

Hall, Timothy L. *Separating Church and State: Roger Williams on Church and State*. Urbana: University of Illinois Press, 1998.

Hamburger, Philip. *Separation of Church and State*. Cambridge, Mass.: Harvard University Press, 2002.

Hanson, R. Scott. *City of Gods: Religious Freedom, Immigration, and Pluralism in Flushing, Queens*. Foreword by Martin E. Marty. New York: Fordham University Press, 2016.

Harrington, R. Ward. "Speaking Scripture: The Flushing Remonstrance of 1657." *Quaker History* 82 (Fall 1993), 104–9.

Hendricks, Obery M., Jr. *Christians Against Christianity: How Right-Wing Evangelicals Are Destroying Our Nation and Our Faith*. Boston: Beacon Press, 2022.

Holmes, David L. *The Faiths of the Founding Fathers*. New York: Oxford University Press, 2006.

Howe, Mark DeWolfe. *The Garden and the Wilderness: Religion and Government in American Constitutional History*. Chicago: University of Chicago Press, 1965.

Hutson, James H., ed. *The Founders on Religion: A Book of Quotations*. Princeton, N.J.: Princeton University Press, 2005.

———. *Religion and the New Republic: Faith in the Founding of America*. Lanham, Md.: Rowman & Littlefield, 2000.

Kaylor, Brian, and Beau Underwood. *Baptizing America: How Mainline Protestants Helped Build Christian Nationalism*. Des Peres, Mo.: Chalice Press, 2024.

Ketchum, Ralph, ed. *Selected Writings of James Madison*. Indianapolis: Hackett, 2006.

Klinkhamer, Marie Carolyn. "The Blaine Amendment of 1875: Private Motives for Political Action." *Catholic Historical Review* 42 (April 1956), 15–49.

Kramnick, Isaac, and R. Laurence Moore. *Godless Citizens in a Godly Republic: Atheists in American Public Life*. New York: W. W. Norton, 2019.

———. *The Godless Constitution: A Moral Defense of the Secular State*. New York: W. W. Norton, 2005.

Lambert, Frank. *The Founding Fathers and the Place of Religion in America*. Princeton, N.J.: Princeton University Press, 2003.

Larson, Edward J. *A Magnificent Catastrophe: The Tumultuous Election of 1800, America's First Presidential Campaign*. New York: Free Press, 2007.

Lutz, Donald S. *Colonial Origins of the American Constitution: A Documentary History*. Indianapolis: Liberty Fund, 1998.

Maclear, J. F., ed. *Church and State in the Modern Age: A Documentary History*. New York: Oxford University Press, 1995.

Maika, Dennis J. "Commemoration and Context: The Flushing Remonstrance Then and Now." *New York History* 89 (Winter 2008), 28–42.

McLoughlin, William G. "Isaac Backus and the Separation of Church and State in America." *American Historical Review* 71 (June 1968), 1392–413.

———, ed. *Isaac Backus on Church, State, and Calvinism: Pamphlets, 1754–1789.* Cambridge, Mass.: Harvard University Press, 1968.

Meacham, Jon. *American Gospel: God, the Founding Fathers, and the Making of a Nation.* New York: Random House, 2006.

Miller, Paul D. *The Religion of American Greatness: What's Wrong with Christian Nationalism.* Lisle, Ill.: IVP Academic, 2024.

Miller, Perry. *Roger Williams: His Contribution to the American Tradition.* Indianapolis: Bobbs-Merrill, 1953.

Moore, James P., Jr. *Prayer in America: A Spiritual History of Our Nation.* New York: Doubleday, 2005.

Morgan, Edmund S. *Roger Williams: The Church and the State.* New York: W. W. Norton, 1967.

Mulder, John M. "William Livingston: Propagandist Against Episcopacy." *Journal of Presbyterian History* 54 (1976), 83–104.

Muñoz, Phillip. "James Madison's Principle of Religious Liberty." *American Political Science Review* 91 (February 2003), 17–32.

Nelson, Anne. *Shadow Network: Media, Money, and the Secret Hub of the Religious Right.* New York: Bloomsbury, 2019.

Newmann, Elizabeth. *Kingdom of Rage: The Rise of Christian Extremism and the Path Back to Peace.* New York: Worthy Books, 2024.

Nussbaum, Martha C. *Liberty of Conscience: In Defense of America's Tradition of Religious Equality.* New York: Basic Books, 2008.

———. *The New Religious Intolerance: Overcoming the Politics of Fear in an Anxious Age.* Cambridge, Mass.: Harvard University Press, 2012.

Onuf, Peter S., ed. *Jeffersonian Legacies.* Charlottesville: University Press of Virginia, 1993.

Peterson, Merrill D., ed. *The Portable Thomas Jefferson.* New York: Penguin Books, 1975.

Pointer, Richard W. *Protestant Pluralism and the New York Experience: A Study of Eighteenth-Century Diversity.* Bloomington: Indiana University Press, 1988.

Ragosta, John A. *Wellspring of Liberty: How Virginia's Religious Dissenters Helped to Win the American Revolution and Secured Religious Liberty.* New York: Oxford University Press, 2010.

Rogers, Melissa. *Faith in American Public Life.* Foreword by E. J. Dionne, Jr. Waco, Tex.: Baylor University Press, 2019.

Sanford, Charles B. *The Religious Life of Thomas Jefferson.* Charlottesville: University Press of Virginia, 1984.

Sehat, David. *The Myth of American Religious Freedom.* New York: Oxford University Press, 2010.

Seidel, Andrew L. *The Founding Myth: Why Christian Nationalism Is Unamerican.* New York: Union Square, 2021.

Skillen, James W., ed. *The School-Choice Controversy: What Is Constitutional?* Grand Rapids, Mich.: Baker Books, 1993.

Smith, Gary Scott. *Faith and the Presidency: From George Washington to George W. Bush.* New York: Oxford University Press, 2006.

Stewart, Katherine. *The Power Worshippers: Inside the Dangerous Rise of Religious Nationalism.* New York: Bloomsbury, 2022.

Sullivan, Winnifred Fallers. *The Impossibility of Religious Freedom.* Princeton, N.J.: Princeton University Press, 2005.

Throckmorton, Warren, and Michael Coulter. *Getting Jefferson Right: Fact-Checking Claims About Thomas Jefferson.* Grove City, Pa.: Salem Grove Press, 2023.

Waldman, Steven. *Founding Faith: How Our Founding Fathers Forged a Radical New Approach to Religious Liberty.* New York: Random House, 2008.

Wenger, Tisa. *We Have a Religion: The 1920s Pueblo Indian Dance Controversy and American Religious Freedom.* Chapel Hill: University of North Carolina Press, 2014.

Wallis, Jim. *The False White Gospel: Rejecting Christian Nationalism, Reclaiming True Faith, and Refounding Democracy.* New York: St. Martin's, 2024.

West, Thomas G. *Vindicating the Founders: Race, Sex, Class, and Justice in the Origins of America.* Lanham, Md.: Rowman & Littlefield, 1997.

Whitehead, Andrew L. *American Idolatry: How Christian Nationalism Betrays the Gospel and Threatens the Church.* Grand Rapids, Mich.: Brazos Press, 2023.

Wilson, John F. *Public Religion in American Culture.* Philadelphia: Temple University Press, 1979.

———. *Religion and the American Nation: Historiography and History.* Athens: University of Georgia Press, 2003.

Wilson, John F., and Donald L. Drakeman, eds. *Church and State in American History: Key Documents, Decisions, and Commentary from the Past Three Centuries.* 3rd ed. Boulder, Colo.: Westview Press, 2003.

ACKNOWLEDGMENTS

The impetus for this book was a brief lunch at the Hanover Inn on October 10, 2018. Having read some of my commentaries over the years, Chip Fleischer invited me to set down a few thoughts about the separation of church and state and its importance in American life. I agreed to think it over, and then, following an unexpected hiatus for medical reasons, the project came together. I'm grateful to Chip for his fine editorial direction and to his colleagues at Steerforth Press for their expertise in shepherding this project to completion.

My wife, the estimable Catharine Randall, is a far better scholar than I. On many evenings after a day of writing, she invited me to read what I had produced. She was unstinting with both her criticisms and her encouragement. I cannot imagine life without her, my best friend.

My colleagues in the religion department at Dartmouth have provided support and a congenial intellectual community, especially during my six-year tenure as department chair. I also want to thank my associate dean, Barbara Will, for her friendship, her encouragement, and for backing me up whenever I launched into yet another tiresome rant about the importance of scholarship in the humanities. I'm grateful also to David Hollinger and Steven J. Green for their careful reading of the manuscript; I alone bear responsibility for any mistakes that remain.

When I began doctoral studies in 1980, I vowed that I would never allow my scholarship to become so recondite that I could not communicate with a general audience. I began contributing op-eds to my hometown newspaper, the *Des Moines Register*, during my graduate school years, and I have sustained that discipline of writing for newspapers ever since. When I left New York for Hanover, New Hampshire, in 2012, I was able to find a home with our very fine local newspaper, the *Valley News*, and eventually also with the *Concord Monitor* and still later with the *Santa Fe New Mexican*. The opportunity to contribute regularly to these papers allowed me the luxury of trying out new ideas, some of which have been developed in these pages. I want to acknowledge a succession of editors at the *Valley News*, most recently Alex Hanson, as well as Jonathan Van Vleet at the *Monitor* and Inez Russell Gomez at the *New Mexican*.

The life of a graduate student offers many enticements and diversions; I shudder to think what I proposed as my field of study when I applied for admission. Fortunately, my mentor, John F. Wilson, provided astute, yet gentle, guidance. When he asked one day if I'd like to assist him with a project examining the relationship between church and state in America, I jumped at the chance — not because I knew much about the topic or had even thought much about it, but because it offered me the opportunity to work with one of the experts in the field.

Long after I left Princeton, John continued to provide astute, gentle guidance. When I asked if he would read a very early draft of this manuscript, he readily agreed, offering crucial suggestions that helped to frame the argument. I have occasionally joked over the years that, because of my undistinguished academic record, I was admitted to Princeton because of a clerical error. John chuckled dismissively whenever I mentioned that — "Oh, Randy!" — but he never denied it.

I have spent much of my career trying to prove — first to myself, then to others — that he did not make a mistake in taking a chance on me all those years ago. To say that I owe John F. Wilson an incalculable debt would be an understatement. The dedication of this book represents a small attempt to discharge that obligation.

ABOUT THE AUTHOR

Randall Balmer (PhD, Princeton University), a prizewinning historian and Emmy Award nominee, is the John Phillips Professor in Religion at Dartmouth College, the oldest endowed chair at the college. Before coming to Dartmouth in 2012, he was professor of American religious history at Columbia University for twenty-seven years, and he has been a visiting professor at Princeton, Yale, Drew, Emory, and Northwestern universities and in the Columbia University Graduate School of Journalism. He is the author of more than a dozen books, including *Evangelicalism in America* and *Redeemer: The Life of Jimmy Carter*. His second book, *Mine Eyes Have Seen the Glory: A Journey into the Evangelical Subculture in America*, now in its fifth edition, was made into a three-part series for PBS. He has written and hosted two other documentaries for PBS, and he is working on another, a history of the Orthodox Church in Alaska. Dr. Balmer's commentaries about religion in America have appeared in newspapers across the country, including the *Los Angeles Times*, the *Des Moines Register*, the *Washington*

Post, the *Santa Fe New Mexican*, and the *New York Times*. In 2024, he received the Martin E. Marty Award for the Public Understanding of Religion from the American Academy of Religion.